Casebooks on Economic Principles

MACROECONOMICS

Andrew Leake
Head of Economics
Latymer Upper School, Hammersmith

Macmillan Education

First published 1982

Published by
MACMILLAN EDUCATION LIMITED
Houndmills Basingstoke Hampshire RG21 2XS
and London
Associated companies throughout the world

Printed in Hong Kong

British Library Cataloguing in Publication Data

Leake, Andrew
Macroeconomics. — (Casebooks on economic principles).
1. Macroeconomics
I. Title
339 HB171

ISBN 0-333-27991-3

Contents

Acknowledgements

The author and publishers wish to thank the following who have kindly given permission for the use of copyright material:

Associated Newspapers Group Limited for an extract 'If Only Denis *did* Know Some Simple Sums' from the *Daily Mail* 14.11.78;

Bank of England for extracts from *The Bank of England Quarterly Bulletin* June 1979;

Club Méditerranée for an extract from their 1979 holiday brochure;

The Controller of Her Majesty's Stationery Office for an extract from *The Attack on Inflation Cmnd. 6151;*

The Daily Telegraph Limited for extracts from the *Daily Telegraph* 'Back to Industrial Investing', 19.6.78; '1970-1977', 30.10.78; 'Lorry Drivers' Test Run' 22.1.79;

David & Charles (Holdings) Limited for extracts from *Cost-Effective Self-Sufficiency or The Middle Class Peasant* by E. & T. McLaughlin (1978);

The Economist Intelligence Unit Limited for an extract from *The Economic Effects of Disarmament* (1963);

The Financial Times Business Information Limited for extracts from *The Financial Times,* 'Tractors', 8.3.78; 'A Money Market Drama', 13.2.78;

Gower Publishing Co. Limited for an extract from *Managing Money and Finance* (2nd edition) by G.P.E. Clarkson and B.J. Elliott;

Midland Bank Limited for an extract from the May 1977 issue of the *Midland Bank Review;*

The Observer Limited for an extract from the *Observer* 'The Future for Jobs' 22.4.79;

Oxford University Press for an extract from 'The Merits of High Wages' in *17th Century Economic Documents* edited by Joan Thirsk and J.P. Cooper (1972);

Punch Publications Limited for a shortened version of an article by E.S. Turner in *Punch* 3.9.75;

Times Newspapers Limited for extracts from articles in the *Sunday Times,* 'Why the world must spend', 10.2.74; 'After the slump, look out for the boom', 23.5.76; and from *The Times,* 'Automation' 13.7.78;

Every effort has been made to trace all the copyright holders but if any have been inadvertently overlooked the publishers will be pleased to make the necessary arrangement at the first opportunity.

1 Introduction

Theory and practice

Learning to drive a car is not easy. You may read all the books, be told what to do by your instructor, and still not be able to do it all by yourself. It takes theory and practice together.

So it is with economics. The theory explains in general terms what should be happening. It takes all possibilities into account. It can be learned from teachers or from textbooks.

For most of us, however, the appeal of economics lies in the practical side of the subject. Just as we want to be able to drive a car for ourselves, so we want to be able to consider and understand the economic problems we see in the real world. It is the purpose of this, and the other Casebooks, to consider theory and practice side by side.

Stage by stage

You have to do many different things to drive a car. You have to control the steering, the accelerator, the brakes and the gears. Although you will use them all together in the end, it helps if you can try them one at a time at the start.

It is the same with economic theory. We need to understand many different ideas, and the connections between them. By taking ideas one at a time, from each area of the subject in turn, we will eventually have built up a complete picture.

So it is the approach in this, and the other Casebooks, to study each important principle in a separate section, and to consider economics stage by stage.

How to use this Casebook

Each section considers a particular aspect of economic behaviour. It does this in three ways. First there is a brief outline of the general principles involved. Next there is an illustration of the way those principles apply in the real world. Finally there are questions based on the issues raised in the section, and arising from the material studied.

The outline of theory is a concise summary of work that has already been covered. It does not develop the general theory to any great depth, but restates and reinforces the most important aspects of each economic principle. It aims to provide a complete preparation for all that follows in the section and in the rest of the Casebook.

The applications are of individual principles rather than of broad topics. Their use will be in making practical sense of abstract ideas and in providing examples to illustrate theoretical points. They are the sort of decisions that are made by individuals and governments each day: things that matter to all of us.

It is hoped that this material will be of interest both for its economic content and in its own right.

Macroeconomics

Macroeconomics is concerned with a particular set of economic problems. It is concerned with economics at a group level — and answers questions about the general levels of activity, employment and prices in any economic system. These are questions that are very different from those that are considered in microeconomics. There we are concerned with individual decisions, as they are taken by buyers and sellers, consumers and producers, and factors of production. In macroeconomics we are interested in the connections between individuals, that bind them all into one economic system. We ask how decisions in one area will affect the situation in quite different areas.

The examples that illustrate the principles of macroeconomics are concerned more with national than with purely individual affairs. The issues that arise are more often the responsibility of government, than of consumers, or firms. Much of the content of this Casebook reflects this.

2 The flow of income

working full time for others. Indeed, were you to become completely self-sufficient, your money income might be almost nothing at all!

Your *real income*, however, would be quite different. Real income is seen in terms of the goods and services themselves, and money payments are not always an accurate measure of that value.

2.1 Income and output

Away from it all

Imagine that you find the courage to 'go self-sufficient'. Your plot of land will be a scene full of rustic wonders, devoted to pigs and potatoes. You will rely, entirely, upon your own food and energy production, but you will work for other people to keep yourself in clothes, transport, entertainment and anything extra you desire.

You will need to work hard at your new occupation. You will have to use your resources — your land, labour, savings — as well as possible. What will happen to your income, as a result?

You will be paid very little money, because you work for others only for a few hours each week, and sell only your surplus produce. Your *money income*, therefore, will be much lower than you could earn by

Real income

You will receive goods and services in payment for two types of work. Work on your own plot of land will produce vegetables, livestock, power, and so forth, which you will consume to be self-sufficient. Work done for others will earn you money, which you will exchange for other types of goods and services produced by the outside world. Your real income is made up of all these products.

Income is, therefore, the same as output. In the exchange economy in the outside world, your own output will be exchanged for other products of equal value that you would prefer to receive as income. Under self-sufficiency, 'the great beauty ... is that the producer is also the consumer'. The same products are both your output, and your income.

If you find more satisfaction from the goods and services you receive by being self-sufficient, the move will clearly have been a wise one: it will have raised your real income.

Away from it all?

Are you tired of the rat race? Do you long to get away from it all — to sell up everything and buy a farm somewhere? Do you want to buck the money system and escape from the throwaway consumer economy? Do you sincerely want to be poor? . . .

However, there is a compromise between remaining a discontented cog in the business machine and sinking your savings in a sea of mud. Stay put and develop your own path. Make your garden, whether it is an estate, a backyard or simply a grow-bag on the patio, into a productive asset, instead of a recurring expense. Rather than working overtime to earn the money to buy convenience foods that are convenient only to the manufacturer, resign yourself to working less hard for other people, and start working for yourself. At least you have more chance of being appreciated.

Don't try to be entirely self-sufficient at first just for the sake of foolish consistency. If your friends point out that you are still dependent on the wicked commercial world for your clothes or cars or carpets, agree with them, and go on saving money on the things you *can* produce for yourself. As you get more

adaptable, the range of these will widen all the time. Concentrate on food production first — this is, after all, the heaviest item of expense for most families — then on the saving of fuel and energy, or even home-production through solar or wind-power. If you can provide these essentials for yourself, you will find that a relatively small amount of paid work will keep you in clothes, transport, entertainment and other home comforts.

. . . The average family of four is reckoned to get a year's vegetables off a plot which measures 30 x 60ft (9 x 18m). But who is 'average'? If your available land is less than this, don't despair because your own requirements may be less too. The great beauty of domestic gardening is that the producer is also the consumer and can forecast very precisely what the family's needs are. If your teenage sons eat around half a hundredweight of potatoes a week, and there is a reasonably cheap source of supply locally, are you going to fill the plot with potatoes, or buy them and grow the pricier, fancy vegetables you would rather eat yourself? One thing to remember is that vegetables straight from the garden taste nicer, so more and more varieties get eaten.

QUESTIONS

(i) How would you expect a change to self-sufficiency to affect your real income for the first few years?

(ii) How would a sale of surplus produce affect your money and real income, under self-sufficiency?

(iii) 'Do you sincerely want to be poor?' Why might you appear to be poor in others' eyes, but not in your own, when you are self-sufficient?

The circular flow of income

There is a circular flow of exchange in any economic system. Under self-sufficiency, you would act as a producer during the working day, to provide goods and services for your consumption out of working hours. This would give you the ability to work as a producer again, the next day.

In a complex economy the exchange between

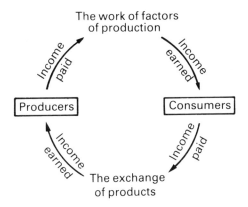

Diagram 1   The circular flow of income

producers and consumers is expressed in terms of payments of money. Producers hire factors of production. Factors earn incomes for consumption. Consumers pay for outputs of goods and services. Each part of the economy is related to every other part through the circular flow of these payments (see diagram 1).

The merits of high wages

A Bristol merchant was arguing, in 1695, for a general rise in the wages of farm workers. This would lead to increased prosperity for all, he claimed, through the circular flow of income.

Higher wages for farm workers would bring higher prices for their products. Those higher prices would cost shopkeepers greater payments, but would increase the rest of their trade, and their profits, even

The merits of high wages

Let us begin with the shopkeeper or buyer and seller, who is the wheel whereon the inland trade turns, as he buys of the importer and manufacturer, and sells again to the country; suppose such a man spends two hundred pounds per annum in all things necessary for his family, both provisions, clothes, house rent, and other expenses, the question will be what proportion of this is laid out in flesh, corn, butter, cheese, etc. barely considered according to their first cost in the market. I presume we shall find fifty or sixty pounds per annum to be the most, and suitably the advance thereon will be about twenty-five to thirty pounds per annum, but the consequence thereof in the profits of his trade will be much more; for by this means the farmer may give a better rent to his landlord, who will be enabled to keep a more plentiful table, spend more wines, fruit, sugars, spices, and other things wherewith he is furnished from the City, wear better clothes, suit himself and his family oftener, and carry on a greater splendour in everything. The farmer according to his condition may do the same, and give higher wages to the labourers employed in husbandry, who might then live more plentifully, and buy new clothes oftener, instead of patching up old. By this means the manufacturer would be encouraged to give a better price for wool, when he should find a vent as fast as he could make; and a flux of wealth causing variety of fashions would add wings to men's inventions, when they shall see their manufactures advanced in their values by the buyer's fancy. This likewise would encourage the merchant to increase his exports, when he shall have a quick vent for his imports; by which regular circulation payments would be short, and all would grow rich. But when trade stops in the fountain, when the gentleman and farmer are kept poor, everyone in his order partakes of the same fate.

more. For higher prices on farm products increase the incomes, and the spending, of farmers, landlords, merchants, and manufacturers, in turn.

Increased spending in one area would be like a fountain (as the extract says), casting benefits on to many others, 'by which regular circulation ... all would grow rich. But when trade stops in the fountain, ... everyone in his order partakes of the same fate.'

QUESTIONS

(i) Find references in the extract to the activities of landlord, and labourer as (a) producer and (b) consumer.

(ii) In the extract, the Bristol merchant describes how 'all would grow rich' as a result of high wages. Is he thinking in terms of money or real income?

2.2 Leakages

The circular flow of income shows that there is a continuing exchange of payments between producers and consumers in the economy. Consumers receive their money income from working as factors of production, and spend it on goods and services produced in the economy. Given long enough, all of their income would be spent in this way, but over any given period of time, some of it may not. Any part of income which is not spent represents a *leakage* from the circular flow of income.

All income must be either spent, as consumption, or not spent, as a leakage. The explanation of how much income is consumed is also the explanation of how much is leaked.

Consumption and savings

To make this clear, we will begin by considering the issue at a personal level. The income available for personal spending could be either consumed or saved. Saving is the only leakage arising from this decision.

The levels of consumption and savings may be influenced by several things, of which the most important is the current level of income. Other things being equal, the level of savings is set by the level of income in the following way.

People first decide how much of their income to spend and whatever is left, is saved. As their income rises, so too will their savings, but not by so much. At the lowest levels of income, people will 'beg, borrow, or steal' to maintain a 'subsistence level' of consumption, and savings will be negative. At higher levels of income, people will save more and more, as their consumption wants are satisfied.

These ideas are represented in the savings line drawn in diagram 1. The slope of that line shows the change in savings (ΔS) when there is a change in income (ΔY). This measure is called the marginal propensity to save (MPS $= \dfrac{\Delta S}{\Delta Y}$).

Disarmament

In the early 1960s the British government were considering a reduction in defence spending. This would allow them to reduce taxation by the same amount and to transfer income from the government, back to private households. Even if the same overall amount of income were to be spent, this would bring a change in consumption, away from products used for defence, and towards products giving personal satisfaction.

In addition, however, it would seem likely that the transfer of income would change the general levels of consumption and savings in the economy. Previously, the government had been spending all the income. How much of it would private consumers choose to spend and to save?

The marginal propensity to save

We would expect an increase in income to increase savings, but not by as much. By how much will be measured by the marginal propensity to save (MPS). The figures in table 1 allow us to estimate the MPS for the time in question. Between 1958 and 1959 it was:

$$\text{MPS} = \frac{\Delta S}{\Delta Y} = \frac{1\,012 - 853}{16\,933 - 16\,074} = 0.2 \text{ (approximately)}$$

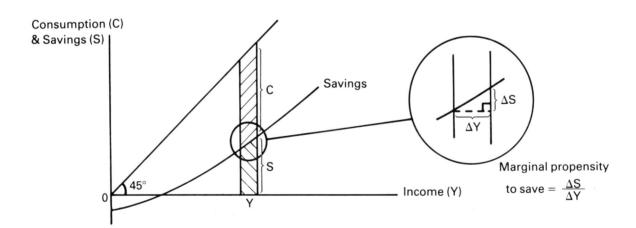

Diagram 1   The savings line

Disarmament

In the event of disarmament an increase in consumers' expenditure would be an obvious means of replacing a proportion of the demand arising from defence. The addition of, for example, £500 million to the total of personal disposable income for 1961 would represent an increase of 2.6 per cent, and if the whole sum were spent it would increase 1961 expenditure by 2.9 per cent. . . . .

If the additional £500 million were distributed to consumers in general through measures of income tax relief, however, it is probable that consumers would decide to save a proportion of the addition to their incomes. . . .

The average marginal propensity to save over the last ten years has been 0.3. The sharp increase in 1960 can be partly accounted for by official discouragement of consumers' expenditure, particularly through hire purchase restrictions, and to this extent consumers would be less likely to save the addition to their incomes if it were distributed at a time when restrictions were relaxed. It can nevertheless also be argued that as consumers become more prosperous they will choose to devote a higher proportion of income to life assurance and other forms of saving, and that this new trend towards a higher rate of saving may be a permanent one. American experience tends to contradict this belief, since personal savings in the U.S. in 1960 amounted to 6.5 per cent of personal disposable income, as compared to 8.8 per cent in the U.K. American savings per head, however, stood at £45, having fallen from over £50 in 1960, while savings per head in the U.K. stood at £30 in 1960 and rose to just over £39 in 1961. A further increase of some £300 million would have been needed in 1961 in order to bring savings per head to the American level for 1960.

On the assumption that the average marginal propensity to save of the last ten years would operate in the year in which the additional £500 million were distributed, the amount saved would be in the region of £150 million and the amount spent in the region of £350 million. The main purpose of redistributing defence expenditure to consumers would to some extent be defeated, since the whole of the demand arising from this proportion of defence expenditure would not be replaced. If it had been decided, therefore, that exactly £500 million of defence demand should be replaced by demand for consumer goods and services, and that this demand should be stimulated by means of tax reliefs, it would be necessary for the government to forego some £710 million in revenue in order to make sure that consumers' expenditure rose by £500 million.

Between 1960 and 1961 it was:

$$\text{MPS} = \frac{\Delta S}{\Delta Y} = \frac{2072 - 1594}{19\,374 - 18\,207} = 0.4 \text{ (approximately)}$$

Clearly its value fluctuates a good deal, but 'the average . . . over the last ten years has been 0.3.'

Table 1   Consumer income, expenditure, and savings 1958-61

Year	Total personal disposable income (current prices) [£ million]	Consumers' expenditure (current prices) [£ million]	Personal savings (current prices) [£ million]
1958	16 074	15 221	853
1959	16 933	15 921	1012
1960	18 207	16 613	1594
1961	19 374	17 302	2072

[Source: Central Statistical Office]

The effects

If consumers chose to save 30% when their income increased by, say, £500 million, then the 'amount saved would be in the region of £150 million and the amount spent in the region of £350 million'. Should the government wish to maintain the level of spending in the economy at the original level of £500 million, they would need to increase personal disposable income by $(£500 \times \frac{100\%}{70\%})$ which is 'some £710 million'.

How would this policy of disarmament have affected the 1961 level of savings? At a level of personal disposable income of £19 374 million, personal savings amounted to £2072 million. If income increased to £19 874 million, then, other things being equal, savings would rise to £2222 million.

QUESTIONS

(i)   The marginal propensity to consume (MPC) is the change in consumption divided by the change in income which caused it. Calculate the MPC (a) between 1959 and 1960, (b) on average over the 10 years up to 1961.

(ii)   Draw a 'savings line' diagram to show the effect upon income and savings that the disarmament policy described in the text would have had in 1961.

(iii)   Suggest a reason why the level of personal savings per head in 1960 and 1961 was greater in the USA than in the UK.

(iv)   Assume that the MPS in the UK in 1961 was 0.4. What would the levels of personal consumption and savings become, following an increase in personal disposable income of £500 million in that year?

(v)   Explain why hire purchase restrictions should increase the level of savings, as in 1960. What effect would this have on the 'savings line'?

Taxation and imports

All personal disposable income will be spent on consumption unless it is leaked from the circular flow of income, in savings. Some income, however, may already have been leaked from the flow, before it was put at the disposal of private individuals — in *direct taxation*. Some of the rest of the income, when it is paid in exchange for consumption goods may also be leaked from the flow: spending on *imports* will take income away from producers within the economy, and payments of *indirect taxation* will take income away again, to the government.

There are, therefore, three different types of leakage. Income earned by factors of production may be spent on the output of producers, or it may be saved, taxed, or spent on imports (see diagram 2).

Each leakage will rise with income, in a similar way to savings, and by how much will be measured in its respective marginal propensity. The marginal propensity to leak (MPL) is found from the addition of the three individual figures, and is directly related to the marginal propensity to consume domestic output (MPC). All extra income goes either in consumption, or leakages (i.e. MPC + MPL = 1).

The multiplier

The circular flow of income implies that any change in income will always cause a 'chain reaction' of further changes. Income that is spent on consumption will generate more income, and the greater the MPC, the more this will happen.

The *multiplier* measures the amount by which income increases as a result of this chain reaction. Its value depends directly upon how much income is passed on in consumption, at each stage of the cycle, in the following way:

$$\text{The multiplier} = \frac{\text{total change in income}}{\text{original change in income}}$$

$$= \frac{1}{1 - \text{MPC}} = \frac{1}{\text{MPL}}$$

There will be no multiplier effect only if all extra income is leaked. There will be an infinitely large multiplier if extra income is consumed totally and immediately. Normally, the multiplier will be between these extremes, and something greater than one in value.

It will be assumed, in the case of the 'disarmament' example, that none of the £500 million was previously being spent, and that savings were the only leakage. The value of the multiplier would then have been $(\frac{1}{\text{MPL}} = \frac{1}{0.3} =)$ $3\frac{1}{3}$, and the eventual rise of national income as a result of increased personal incomes would have been (£500 million × $3\frac{1}{3}$ =) £1667 million (approximately).

Why the world must spend its way out of trouble

There were two major changes that affected world economies in 1974. There was first a shortage, and then a four-fold rise in the price of oil. From the point of view of oil-importing countries such as Britain, this resulted in a large rise in the amount of income being paid for imports.

In addition, there was a change in the policy of the government, both in Britain and in many other countries. Concerned about the inflationary effects of the

Income received
from firms as payments
to factors of production,
over a given period of time.

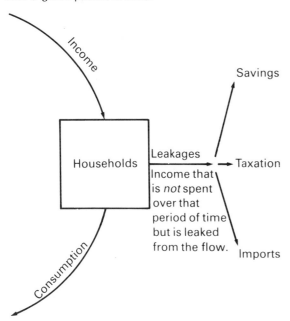

Income spent on consumption,
on output of goods
& services by firms,
over a given period of time.

Diagram 2   Consumption and leakages

Why the world must spend its way out of trouble

The Christmas Budget, which aimed to cut demand by about ½% of the total national product, was predicated on oil shortages persisting throughout the year. If this had remained the most probable outlook, it would have spelled shortages of most kinds of goods as well. Industrial capacity would therefore have been reduced, requiring a tough Budget to balance demand and supply. . . .

The price increases of oil have exactly the opposite effect to that of the production cutbacks, on the balance of supply and demand in the economies of the developed countries. In the absence of offsetting measures, the price increase (less the feedback to British exports which the increased oil payments will stimulate to some extent) has precisely the same effect on our real incomes as an increase in UK Customs duties on oil products, of about £1,500m a year. (Say, £1,850m a year in price increases, less £350m in induced exports to oil-exporting countries.) Therefore, adding the Budget's deflationary measures to those of the oil sheikhs, measures have been taken to cut demand in the UK of some £2,500m a year. . . .

There are, moreover, phenomena called multipliers, which British economists nowadays tend to overlook – for good reason, even though it was a Briton who invented the concept. The "multiplier" means that any change in demand gets multiplied up, through chain reactions on employment and consumption. Any such change occurring in Britain alone – any policy measure or major chance event affecting output and employment – is normally subject to a very low multiplier because much of the effects "leak out" through compensating changes in exports and imports.

But the effects of the oil price increases impinge on the whole world. Many economists under-estimated the world-wide boom in 1973, because the multiplier effects were very large, most of the industrial countries having adopted expansionary policies at the same time. Likewise, in a downward direction, there is a danger that the depressing effects of the oil price increases (on real incomes, output and employment) could turn out to be a high multiple (possibly 6 or 7) of their direct impact, which is usually put at around $50,000m. . . .

So unless governments abroad take the necessary reflationary measures, we may be standing on the brink of the worst recession since the war.

---

oil price rises, these governments introduced budget measures to reduce demand. In large part, these measures took the form of tax increases.

At the same time, therefore, there were large increases in the amount of income taken by each of the leakages, imports and taxation. These changes brought a corresponding reduction in the consumption demand for home-produced goods and services, to the extent of 'some £2500 million a year' in the UK, and 'around $50 000 million' world-wide.

These effects will have caused the further chain reaction of the multiplier process. With reduced income available for spending on goods other than oil, each country will have found it more difficult to sell to its neighbours. Consumption and income will have fallen by much more than the initial rise in oil payments, although by how much would depend upon the value of the relevant multiplier.

In the UK, where the marginal propensities to save, tax, and import are relatively high, little income is passed on in consumption on each circuit of the circular flow of income. In the oil-importing world at large, it seems likely that the multiplier effect will be greater, especially if the policy responses of governments are included as an effect of the oil price change.

Economists are often criticised, as are the weather-forecasters, for their inaccuracy in predicting future events. In this example, it is a matter of grim satisfaction to record that the prediction of 'the worst recession since the war' was all too accurate!

QUESTIONS

(i) The oil-exporting countries were expected to increase their income from the UK by £1850 million a year, but to increase their purchases of UK goods and services by only £350 million. What was their marginal propensity to import from the UK?

(ii) Suggest two changes, other than reflationary measures by governments in oil-importing countries, that might have prevented the risk of recession, following the oil price rise.

(iii) Assume that the value of the multiplier in the oil-importing world was 6. What was the value of the marginal propensity to leak?

(iv) Suggest three changes that would increase the value of the multiplier in the UK.

(v) Assume that the MPC in the UK was 0.25. Use the statistics in the extract to estimate the overall change in UK national income, that would result from the Christmas Budget and the oil price rise, together.

2.3 Injections

Producers sell their output of goods and services to meet the demands of buyers in the economy. Buyers finance their spending from the income they have earned by working as factors of production. All spending will be paid for from income, but not necessarily over the same period of time. Any part of spending which is not paid for from current income represents an *injection* into the circular flow of income.

Demand throughout the economy, therefore, arises from either consumption or injection spending. Injections can be for investment, government spending or exports. None of these forms of demand will be influenced by the current level of income within

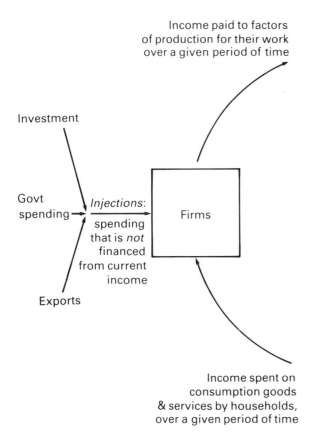

Diagram 1   Consumption and injections

the economy, but rather, by income at a different time, in a different place, or by issues other than income altogether. Their explanation therefore, is generally quite different from that for leakages (see diagram 1).

The government will decide how much it wishes to spend on the basis of its various policies. In the main these will be social or political in nature. Exports will be decided by the spending of people in different economies, and will be based on income elsewhere. Investment plans will be based on several considerations, which are studied in more detail in what follows.

Back to industrial investing?

Investment spending is on particular types of goods. Machines, buildings, and other items of capital are products that do not provide immediate satisfaction to consumers, but are themselves used by firms to produce more goods and services in the future.

Firms will plan to spend on investment goods if they expect to make a profit from doing so. This is only possible if they expect to gain more in returns than they will lose in costs. Between them, the levels of costs and returns explain the rate of planned industrial investment.

Costs and returns

Funds for investment must be borrowed on loan or supplied from a firm's own resources. In either case, the opportunity cost of using those funds will be reflected in market rates of interest, and the higher the rates, the greater the cost of investment.

'Low interest rates' may not affect business management directly, or in the short-term, but they will have an influence upon 'the terms on which companies can raise new capital'.

An investor will predict, as accurately as possible, the returns he expects to gain from his investment in the future. If 'prospective levels of consumption' are high, then his 'likely sales revenue' will lead him to expect high returns from investment. When business expectations are poor, there will be less demand for investment goods.

Since profitability sets the demand for investment, it is possible for the government to influence its level. Policies that reduce costs and raise expectations of future returns will encourage 'a full healthy amount of capital investment'.

The accelerator

Investment plans depend upon 'estimates of the market for the product', and on 'prospective levels of consumption'. This is especially true of investment that is in extra machinery, of a conventional type. It is only when output needs to be expanded, in order to meet an increase in the level of consumption, that the demand for such investment arises. This connection between the change in consumption demand, and the level of investment demand is known as the *accelerator principle*.

Tractors

Farmers invest in extra tractors in order to be able to improve their production of crops. The boom in crop sales in 1972 encouraged them to 'press ahead with new investment', and brought an 'accelerated' rise in tractor sales. The levelling off in the consumption demand for crops after 1976 'eroded business confidence', and reduced this type of demand to a minimum.

Tractors

At present, manufacturers are treating the fall in demand fairly calmly, pointing out that the downturn is from an unexpectedly high level. The past boom can be traced to 1972, about the time of the intervention by the Soviet Union to buy up the United States' grain surplus. Farm commodity shortages led to higher prices, which attracted more land into cultivation and placed new demands upon the agricultural equipment suppliers. In the U.K., profits from potatoes and other crops gave farmers the funds and the confidence to press ahead with new investment to push tractor sales to a record 38,381 units in 1976 — well above the forecast trend for the current decade of just over 30,000 vehicles a year.

But, as suppliers to a cyclical industry like agriculture, the tractor manufacturers have learned to live with sudden swings in demand. From a position of running plants near to full capacity, overtime working, and long delivery delays, companies are now having to fight for orders and to cut production programmes. Good harvests in 1976, and consequent large stocks, particularly in North America, have held down world prices of wheat and feed grains, reduced farmers' liquidity, and eroded investment confidence. To the downturn of demand from the advanced western economies must be added the political and economic uncertainties which hamper sales to the developing nations.

The effect on producers of the investment good (tractors) of changes in the output of consumption goods (crops) is clearly a significant one. Despite the continuing demand for tractors due to other types of investment, the level of spending has changed a great deal. Producers in an investment goods industry such as tractors, have to 'learn to live with sudden swings in demand'.

QUESTIONS

(i)   Explain how 'profitability, present and prospective' will affect the costs and returns from investment.

(ii)   Suggest two reasons why a farmer might buy a tractor, other than to increase crop production.

(iii)   Explain why an investment goods industry will suffer from 'sudden swings in demand' more than a consumption goods industry.

(iv)   Suggest two policies the government of a developing nation might introduce to increase its farmers' investment in tractors.

(v)   Suggest two ways in which the changes in the UK economy in 1974 (see page 10) might have affected the demand for investment goods.

3 Output

3.1 Explaining the level of output

A modest revival in output

There was a 'modest revival' in the level of output in the economy towards the end of 1976. The main cause seems to have been 'a reduction of savings relative to investment spending'. If so, how did this lead to a rise in output?

The explanation follows from the ideas of the circular flow of income, leakages, and injections.

A modest revival in output

The modest revival towards the end of 1976 seems to have sprung from a reduction of savings relative to investment spending in the private sector, or in other words from a reduction in the size of its financial surplus. The strongest expansionary influence was a sharp reduction in the personal savings ratio, from 15 per cent of disposable income in the first three quarters of the year to 11½ per cent in the last.

The circular flow of income

The flow of payments between consumers and producers in an economy continues indefinitely, but the level of payments can rise or fall from time to time. An increase in the amount of economic activity will increase the money value of national income, which is the same as national output.

Chart 1 shows (if we take the index of industrial production as a measure of output in this case) that the level of output fell in the third quarter of 1976, but rose markedly in the fourth quarter.

Leakages

Other things being equal, the level of leakages will rise with the level of income. There can be leakages of income into savings, taxation and imports, but to simplify matters in this case we will assume that only personal savings have changed.

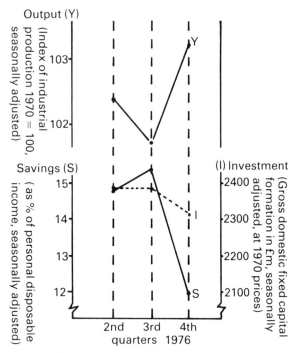

[Source: *Monthly Digest* April 1977]

Chart 1

The change in conditions in the last quarter of 1976 made private individuals much less willing to save at each level of income. Chart 1 shows that 15.5% of personal disposable income was saved in the third quarter, but only 11.6% in the fourth quarter. This will have brought a corresponding rise in consumption spending, well above the usual seasonal increase.

On diagram 1 this change is shown as a *shift* of the leakage line. More would be taken from the circular flow in leakages, at each level of national income.

Injections

Plans for injection spending are not affected by changes in the level of income, but by the various influences considered previously. Here it will again clarify matters to assume that investment spending is the only injection to have been affected by changes at the end of 1976, and that it can be measured in the statistics for gross domestic fixed capital formation.

Chart 1 shows that the level of investment fell in real terms towards the end of 1976, but only slightly.

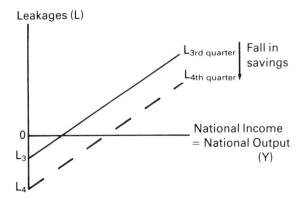

Diagram 1   A shift in leakages

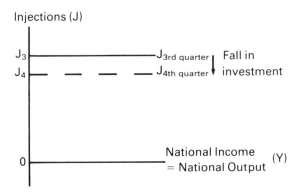

Diagram 2   A shift in injections

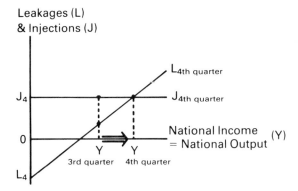

Diagram 3   The equilibrium process

This change is illustrated, in terms of an injection line, in diagram 2. Changes from high to low levels of current income do not affect the level of planned injection spending, but the reduction in investment intentions is seen as a downward shift at all levels of income.

The equilibrium process

There is an automatic process that will tend to balance the levels of leakages and injections in the economy at any one time. It has been shown how leakage and injection plans are decided separately and differently, but now we can see how the two are matched: through changes in national income.

Injections add to the level of income in the circular flow and leakages subtract from it. If injections begin by being greater than leakages, then more is being put into the circular flow of income than is being taken from it. The level in the flow will tend to rise. As it rises, injections will *not* be affected but leakages will be raised as well. This process will continue so long as injections exceed leakages, but will tend, all the time, to raise leakages to the same level as that for injections. Equilibrium will occur when leakages finally balance injections.

This process is automatic, and works in either direction. It can be seen on diagram 3, as a *move* along both leakage and injection lines, since it assumes that all other influences remain constant. It depends upon changes in national income to lead the economy to its equilibrium level. This equilibrium level is then the level of output in the economy.

Output in 1976

If this equilibrium process works from beginning to end within each quarter, we can now explain the change in output towards the end of 1976.

Between the third and fourth quarter, investment fell slightly, but the savings line shifted so that much less was saved at each level of income. (This change is shown in the comparison of diagrams 1 and 2.)

The 'reduction of savings relative to investment spending' caused more to be injected into the circular flow than was being withdrawn from it. The level of output, therefore, rose from an index of 101.5 to 103.2 over the quarter, and the economy generally showed 'a modest revival'.

QUESTIONS

(i)   Assume, still, that changes have occurred in savings and investment alone. Draw a leakage and injection diagram to explain the change in output between the 2nd and 3rd quarters of 1976.

(ii)   Draw a leakage and injection diagram to show the effect of the changes in taxes, and oil prices, upon the world economy in 1974 (see page 10).

(iii)   Suggest one reason for each of the changes in savings and investment at the end of 1976.

The Kenyan coffee boom

The big commodity boom of coffee and tea, [which] started in 1976, ended up making 1977 an exceptionally good year. The overall growth of the economy was 7.3 per cent and all sectors of the economy experienced phenomenal growth rates. Agricultural sector incomes increased by 12.3 per cent at constant (1972) prices as coffee earnings doubled and those of tea tripled.

The coffee and tea earnings saved the economy from the 1974/75 slump and had their greatest impact on the balance-of-payments position. A surplus of £112.7 million was realised compared to £35.7 million attained in 1976.

Even a surplus in the current account of £24.1 million was realised against deficits in the past 13 years. Overall exports increased by 45.4 per cent in value terms in 1977 and coffee and tea accounted for nearly 60 per cent of the earnings. . . .

Present forecasts are that coffee and tea prices in 1978 will fall by over 30 per cent of the 1977 price level and coffee production may fall by up to 40 per cent.

Thus we can expect a deterioration of the balance-of-payments position in 1978 unless some corrective measures are taken soon. One such corrective measure would be to restrain imports while expansion of exports is pursued. . . .

Now that the boom has come to an end, how was the boom money used? The coffee and tea farmers and those involved in exporting these commodities were the direct beneficiaries but the impact of the boom affected all activities throughout the economy. . . .

The "coffee party" is over.

Last year's bumper earnings, which were immediately transformed into a spending spree by many Kenyans to fuel a new high for domestic inflation, is now giving way to sober stock-taking.

Last year . . . Kenya was riding on the crest of an economic wave which brought a new high in incomes for many Kenyans as the coffee earnings percolated into the other sectors of the economy and generated a multiplier effect in boosting domestic demand. . . .

With the boom, the revival came in the building industry, albeit towards the tailend late last year. But after the coffee money had been spent on buying beer and cars, the farmers quickly realised that they better build something more tangible with the windfall profits. Thus, a real upsurge of buildings in the private sector was noticed in the rural areas.

The Kenyan coffee boom

We will now study in more depth the results of changes in leakages and injections. The rise in export earnings that affected the economy of Kenya in 1977 illustrates many of the issues involved.

The story begins in 1976, with the commodity price boom that raised the prices of most of the products that Kenya was exporting, and of coffee and tea, in particular.

These increases in export earnings — an overall increase of 45.4% in 1977 — represented increased injections of income into the Kenyan economy. It was this rise in injections which caused most of the changes that followed.

Other injections and leakages

It does seem possible, however, that there were other 'shifts' in injections and leakages at the same time. The rise in world prices, for instance, is likely to have increased the amount paid for imports into Kenya, at every level of income.

Changes in the government's policy might have prompted them to introduce changes in their levels of taxation and spending. They will have been concerned over the 'new high for domestic inflation', and the expected 'deterioration of the balance of payments position'. The search for 'corrective measures' to both of these problems would have to include rises in taxation and cuts in government spending.

There might also have been changes in savings and investment. 'A spending spree by many Kenyans' might imply that they chose to spend more of their available income on consumption, and reduced savings at all income levels.

'The revival in the building industry' represents an increase in the level of investment in the economy, which might be due to various influences. If interest rates had fallen, or if the prospects for future prosperity were high, farmers and others would be encouraged to expand their plans for investment. If the rate of consumption demand were increasing, there would be a new demand for investment goods, through the operation of the accelerator.

The circular flow of income

Whatever other changes occurred, there was certainly a large increase in injections from the export earnings. Certain groups of producers would have benefited directly from this increased income, but their spending would have spread the benefits to others in the economy, through the circular flow of income.

In this way, 'coffee earnings percolated into the

other sectors of the economy', as there were successive circuits of earning and spending. The amount passed on to other groups will have depended directly upon the marginal propensity to consume (MPC) of farmers, and of the economy as a whole. Since there was a 'spending spree' — even if it was only on beer and cars at first — it seems likely that the MPC was high, and that the gains were widely spread. This is supported by the fact that 'agricultural sector incomes increased by 12.3%', but that the economy as a whole also managed to grow by as much as 7.3%.

The multiplier

The circulation of export earnings to other sectors of the economy 'brought a new high in incomes for many Kenyans'. The final rise in income was much greater than the initial rise in earnings from exports, because of the multiplier effects of the changes. Farmers spent their increased income, and kept other producers — selling beer and cars for instance — in income and employment. If their 'spending spree' was particularly enthusiastic, their marginal propensity to consume, and so also the multiplier, would have been especially high.

The level of output

It will be assumed here that the improvement in the balance of payments was the only change in leakages and injections between 1976 and 1977, and due entirely to exports. Demand increased therefore by (£112.7 million − £35.7 million =) £77.0 million in the Kenyan economy, and brought about a multiplied rise in equilibrium output.

When injections exceeded leakages, national income began to rise, so raising the level of leakages. This process continued, as shown in diagram 4, until leakages balanced injections at the increased level of income set in 1977.

Much of this rise in national income will have been due to a rise in real output — in terms of beer, cars, buildings, etc. Some of it, however, was clearly no more than a monetary change, due to a rise in the general level of prices, and a 'new high for domestic inflation'.

QUESTIONS

(i)   Assuming *no* changes in policy, how would you have expected the coffee boom to have affected the budget (government spending and taxation) of the Kenyan government?

(ii)   Which of the 'possible other changes' in leakages and injections described in the text would lead national income, other things being equal, to (a) rise and (b) fall?

(iii)   Assume that the MPC for the Kenyan economy was 0.75. What would be the rise in national income following increased injections of £77 million?

(iv)   Under what circumstances would the increase in injections cause only an *equal* rise in national income?

(v)   Draw a leakage and injection diagram to show the effect of the forecast prices for coffee and tea upon Kenyan national income in 1978, other things being equal.

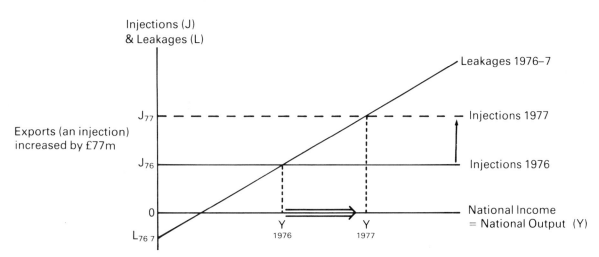

Diagram 4   A boom in national output

3.2 Living standards

In order to compare the standard of living in different economies, or at different times, it is necessary to have a means of measurement. The most complete measure possible will be based upon the level of income in the economy, which results from the interaction of leakages and injections.

The Kenyan coffee boom, for instance, increased national income a good deal in 1977. Measurements of national income and output will show by how much. In addition, however, it would be necessary to consider other issues that affect living standards, in order to see how far that rise in money income reflected a real benefit to the people of Kenya.

We can consider these issues most clearly by returning to a more simple type of economy, where a household has 'gone self-sufficient' in certain forms of production, but trades with the outside world in everything else. We must ask two questions: how is it possible to measure the income of this household before and after its move to self-sufficiency; and what else must be known to assess the change in the real living standards of the people in the household?

How to measure money income

Income is the same as output, and the amount generated depends upon the level of economic activity. Each act of economic exchange, each good and service, must be included in the measure of the total income, and this is only possible if money is used as a common unit of account. Total money income is found from the addition of the money values of each type of output in the economy.

Due to the circular flow of payments, these same money values can be measured in different ways and yet produce a common answer. The money value of the income of factors will match the money value of the output of firms, and the money value of spending on goods and services. Total income can therefore be measured by the *income, output* or *expenditure* methods.

Does it pay?

Our household economy can use the income method to measure the effect of its change to self-sufficiency. Last year's income was earned only from the work of labour, in employment for other people. This

Does it pay?

The whole enterprise of running a self-sufficient garden is intended to be cost-effective. You will want to check if your personal effort is economically viable, if only to have an answer for idle friends and armchair critics. The only way to do this is to keep a detailed account. . . .

First, extract the annual running expenses. These will be very similar every year and include the cost of the following: packets of seeds, onion sets, seed potatoes, and any annual plants bought in; peat, sand, potting composts, growing bags; fertiliser, insecticides, any other chemicals or treatments; peat and plastic-film pots, fillis, plant ties, natural fibre nets and anything else which doesn't last more than one season; hire of cultivator or other machinery; rent of allotment; charge for metered water there or additional hose rate above the ordinary house water rates; any paid labour for holiday periods; cost of advertisements, hire of stall, packaging etc, for selling surplus produce. In later years, repairs and replacements will also figure in running costs. . . .

Gardening is hard work, done consistently and conscientiously. Some economists insist that you should include in your accounts the cost of your labour. We think this would only be equitable if you were giving up other paid work to do the gardening. . . .

Against all this expenditure, reduced to an annual figure, you should set the value of your produce. This can be worked out quite simply by weighing it as it is harvested and checking the current prices in local shops. Early produce is worth more than main crops, because you would have had to pay more for it at the time.

When you have a surplus of produce, don't include it in the normal accounts at its shop value, if you mean to sell it. You won't get the shop price for it, unless you are a remarkable salesman. . . .

Food which you process should be valued at the equivalent commercial rate, rather than the cost of fresh food. Don't forget to deduct the same poundage from the unprocessed total, if you have included it already. . . .

When you have included every item in your accounts, you will be left with the unquantifiables. How do you cost the value of fresh food as against tired shop food? How do you rate your better health, not only from working out of doors but from eating food which has not been processed commercially or exposed to disease through being handled in markets and shops by people who may be carriers of viruses? How much less have you paid in prescription charges because you don't any longer need drugs to sleep or calm down? How much money have you saved by not driving to the shops for food?

year's income is earned from different sources: from a limited amount of paid employment, from selling surplus produce, and from the direct receipt of the household's own produce.

The money value of the income received from self-production will need to be carefully assessed, from comparable prices in shops and markets. Those prices will only measure the return to the household's own factors of production when payments to factors in the outside world have been deducted.

It will be important to avoid counting income earned from one act of work more than once. *Transfer payments*, such as 'pocket money', are received although no work has been done, and must not be counted as part of total income.

Imaginary figures for the household's income before and after its change are suggested in table 1. They show that money income has remained the same overall although the sources, and types, of that income have changed a good deal.

Real income

Money values are needed to take all types of income, output or expenditure into account on a comparable basis. The overall measure they provide, however, will not reflect the real level of production of goods and services, if the relative value of money itself changes.

A rise in the general level of prices, for instance, will increase the money value of goods and services, even if there has been no rise in real output. If money income is the same this year as last, but all prices have risen by 10%, then real income is in fact 10% less than last year (see table 1).

This comparison will prove difficult if some prices change more than others, or income is received in terms more of one good than another. A detailed 'cost of living' index will then be necessary, to assess changes in the relative value of money.

Living standards

From the figures in table 1, the household would so far conclude that its real income, in terms of the value of the goods and services it has received, has fallen as a result of 'going self-sufficient'. It will need, however, to take other issues into consideration.

It may prefer the types of products that make up its income now: 'fresh food as against tired shop food'. It may find benefits in things that are not quantifiable as goods and services at all: better health or more independence. It may prefer a more even distribution of income, and effort, within the household, and find that this is achieved through self-sufficiency. If these issues bring gains that outweigh

Table 1   Does it pay? (imaginary figures)

	LAST YEAR (working full-time for other people.)	THIS YEAR (when semi-'self-sufficient.')
MONEY INCOME	(£000)	(£000)
Income to Labour, from working for other people	8	4
Income to Land, Labour, Capital and Enterprise, from selling produce to others	0	1
Income to Land, Labour, Capital, and Enterprise, from working under 'self-sufficiency'	0	3
	8	8
REAL INCOME		
Relative loss in real income if all prices rose by 10% between last year and this year	0	0.8
	8	7.2
LIVING STANDARDS		
Other issues to consider: The types of products received as income; benefits received but unquantifiable as income; etc.,	A loss?	A gain?
		Change in overall living standards . . . A gain from 'going self-sufficient'?

any tangible losses of income, self-sufficiency may yet raise the living standards of the household.

QUESTIONS

(i)   Expenditure method: suggest examples of spending in our 'self-sufficiency economy' on (a) domestic consumption, (b) investment, (c) exports, (d) imports.

(ii)   Output method: explain how this economy will calculate the 'value added' by its production activity.

(iii)   Income method: (a) why should any sale of surplus produce *not* be valued at shop prices? (b) how far would the price of produce measure the incomes of factors in the household?

(iv)   Find, from the extract, an example of possible 'double-counting' in the value of production.

(v)   Suggest two examples of how self-sufficiency will change the type of income besides changing 'tired shop food' to fresh food.

4 Employment

4.1 Types of unemployment

Unemployment of factors of production represents a waste of scarce resources, and a failure to satisfy as many consumption wants as possible. This will be of concern to a government which takes responsibility for maintaining an efficient economy.

Unemployment of labour will be of special concern. It will represent, in addition to a neglect of economic resources, a source of social hardship, and political instability. There is, therefore, a particular need to understand the problem, its causes, and possible solutions to it.

The market for labour

Unemployment exists because there are not as many jobs being offered as there are people wishing to work. The demand for labour is less than supply, and the excess of supply is seen as unemployment.

The demand for labour, as with all factors of production, is a derived demand. Firms employ workers in order to produce goods and services which are in demand. The level of demand for labour, therefore, will be set by the level of demand for goods and services.

The supply of labour will be different in different parts of the market, because of the advantages and disadvantages of working in different types of jobs. The supply of labour in the economy as a whole, will change relatively little, and then mainly because of changes in population, or social factors.

An excess of supply over demand would often be expected to lead to a clearing process, through changes in price. In the labour market this process works only slowly and imperfectly, if at all. The price of labour — the wage rate — is kept at a disequilibrium level by a number of imperfections that dominate the market. Even when wages do fall, they might cause a further fall in the demand for labour, and so maintain the imbalance.

For these reasons, unemployment of labour, if ever it is caused by a low level of demand relative to supply, will tend to persist.

Microeconomics and macroeconomics

It is possible to study the behaviour of the market for labour as an individual factor market governed by the microeconomic principles of demand and supply. Indeed, it was generally accepted for many years that the unemployment of labour could be understood entirely in these terms.

There are certainly several types of unemployment which are caused by particular conditions, within individual markets, that are best seen in these terms, but the development of macroeconomics has allowed us to add to this explanation.

It is now possible to explain, and to treat, the unemployment that arises from the connections between different forces in the economy. It is this general type, or 'mass unemployment', that will command most of our interest in what follows. First it is necessary to distinguish it from its fellows.

The future for jobs

Frictional unemployment Workers often change from one job to another, and may become temporarily unemployed in between. Frictional unemployment like this will result in some being out of work although job vacancies are already awaiting them.

The future for jobs will include transfers of workers from one type of work to another — from unskilled work to skilled work, for instance. If there is a 'normal', temporary period of relocation in the meantime, this will be frictional unemployment.

Structural unemployment Changes in the pattern of demand for particular products will bring, as a result, changes in the pattern of demand for workers in particular industries. The relative decline of industries such as steel, ship-building, and textiles causes structural unemployment of their workers.

Since the change is seen in relation to other markets, the forces of supply and demand should introduce an equal rise in labour opportunities elsewhere. There will be growth areas, such as the 'new electronics technology', which, all being well, will absorb the unemployed. A smooth transition from one type of work to another, in line with the changing structure of demand, can be prevented, however, by the different skills and locations required for each job.

Technological unemployment Another transfer of demand for labour can follow the substitution of factors within an industry. 'Investment in better productive systems' will result in technological unemployment for some, but should bring, in addition, a rise in the demand for labour to service the new

The future for jobs

No one has been more surprised by the steady improvement in employment figures over the past year than the Government itself and its forecasters.

By all the traditional rules related to statistics, the rise in the numbers of people coming on to the labour market, the sluggishness of output in the country and the continued problems of main sectors of British industry – all should have led to much higher unemployment.

Yet, instead of the 1.6-1.8 million unemployed which many forecasters had predicted for this time, the total has gone down to 1.3 million and employment has gone up. . . .

Some of the credit can go to specific employment measures. These have grown apace in the past three years. . . .

Their cost has grown too. Some £400 million per year is being spent on direct employment programmes at present. When the panoply of special protection for individual industries, such as steel and shipbuilding, as well as the regional industry grants for employment reasons, are added, the total cost of direct and disguised subsidies to employment could add up to £1 billion, and possibly to £1.5 billion.

But these are essentially defensive schemes. They provide little explanation for the underlying improvement in employment of the last year. Nor, though the Department of Employment claims that it is keeping 176,000 people off the unemployment register at the moment, is there much evidence that the schemes are more than a stop-gap measure. . . .

Employment has increased largely because activity has increased far more than the formal statistics would have it. Everyone has long suspected the force of the cash, or unrecorded, economy. . . .

Within the world of more conventional statistics, too, there has been ample evidence of greater activity and greater creation of jobs than had been predicted.

. . . The steel, shipbuilding, textile, chemical and electrical appliance industries are all facing international pressures, for which the only answer can be a fundamental restructuring and slimming. . . .

The difficulty here is that any policy of renewal suggests lower, not higher, employment as investment goes in better productive systems and new technology. Yet any policy to preserve employment . . . risks intensification of the trend of low productivity which has so marred British performance in the last decades.

The puzzle in the manufacturing sector is that, on most evidence, industry *is* restructuring. The investment figures are high. Companies, from tyres to television tubes, are regrouping their productive forces. Yet overall employment in manufacturing industry has remained surprisingly stable over recent years. More worrying, there is a wide-spread moan, even in industries of greatest contraction such as that of steel, about shortages of skilled labour, particularly in the fields where new electronics technology is most important.

machines, and for labour to operate them. It may be for this reason that 'overall employment . . . has remained surprisingly stable'.

Demand-deficiency unemployment The general level of demand in the economy will affect employment in all industries together. If there is 'greater economic activity', this will lead to a 'greater creation of jobs' throughout. Mass unemployment, caused by a general deficiency of demand, will fall.

Total unemployment

These, and other, causes will each play a part in setting the level of total unemployment. Each of them will be suitable for treatment by different policies of government. Frictional, structural, and technological unemployment are all explained in microeconomic terms, by a change from one pattern of demand for labour to another. 'Mass' unemployment will be explained in macroeconomic terms by the general level of demand for all forms of output throughout the economy.

QUESTIONS

(i) What part have each of the four main types of unemployment played in the fall from 1.6 to 1.3 millions unemployed described in the extract?

(ii) Explain why the changes observed in the 'traditional . . . statistics . . . should have led to much higher unemployment', and illustrate your answer with a demand and supply diagram of the general labour market.

(iii) Suggest four policies that the government could introduce to reduce the level of unemployment caused by each of the four main types described in the text.

4.2 Output and employment

The employment of labour is affected by the level of output in a very direct way. If there is low demand for all types of goods and services, then there will be a low level of output in the economy. This is explained through the interaction of leakages and injections. A low level of output will cause a low level of demand for labour, and general unemployment, of the type described previously as 'demand-deficiency' unemployment. How does this come about?

Automation

The development of the silicon chip, or microprocessor, allows producers to fit mini-computors into a wide range of equipment at relatively little cost. This encourages investment in new technology, in many different fields, on a scale that has led some to call this the 'second industrial revolution'! Some labour markets will lose and others will gain by automation. The labour working for a firm that introduces the new technology will probably be divided into just two such markets. Some workers, presumably the less skilled, who perform routine, manual work, will be substitutes for the new machinery. They will be replaced by it, and become unemployed. Other workers who are skilled, and hired to operate the expensive new machinery, will be complementary to it. The demand for their labour will rise, so increasing their employment and wages.

Amongst the workers directly involved, therefore, there will be a transfer of demand for labour. Employment of unskilled workers will fall and employment of skilled workers will rise. Automation is intended, however, to replace men with machines, and it seems likely, on balance, that jobs will be lost. Technological unemployment will result, but not necessarily on a scale to bring 'a new era of mass unemployment'. That will depend upon the general effects of automation on the economy.

Automation

The most important misunderstanding around seems to be that the introduction of the microprocessor will generate a new era of mass unemployment. It will do this, it is argued, by destroying jobs in manufacturing industry as automation spreads. . . .

Take the issue of laws designed to make it easier for women, or minority ethnic groups, to find work. These laws are often opposed or at least suspected by unions on the grounds that the groups who gain, such as women, will be "stealing" jobs from men.

The truth is very different and, unusually for economics, rather more encouraging. Take the case of women entering the workforce who were not employed before. They will produce goods and earn pay. The pay they earn will enable them to buy things which they otherwise would not have bought; indeed it may even force them to buy some sorts of consumer goods to give them time to play their part in running the home and holding down a job at the same time.

The net effect of women going out to work is thus not to increase unemployment among men; it is to cause some men to lose jobs in some occupations and to find work in others, perhaps in making the dishwashing machines that the affluence of a two-income family can afford.

There may, of course, be problems in the labour market itself as these new workers enter it prepared to accept a lower level of pay. But even that problem does not cause unemployment. Lower real wages mean either higher profits, which are income for someone in the form of dividends, or lower prices, which mean higher real wages for people in other sectors of the economy. The only way in which unemployment could result would be if demand consistently fell below supply. . . .

The same sort of analysis applies to the introduction of a new cheaper form of machine which boosts the productivity of the labour force. One possibility (not a very likely one admittedly) is that it will just push up the wages of workers operating the new machines (for example a machine tool controlled by a micro-computer) to such a high level that the real cost of the product being turned out remains the same.

If that happens, all the benefits of the new technology will go to those still employed in the industries but the rest of us need not be worse off.

The rest of us will be employed in occupations which, to some extent, have come into existence to meet the demands of the new breed of super-rich working in the automated factories. They will have to spend their money or to save it.

If they spend it the level of demand is maintained. In so far as they save it either the private market will find new investments to use the money or the Government has the scope and duty to provide the extra demand, either through cutting taxes on the rest of society who are prepared to spend the money which they earn, or through increasing public spending which provides both welfare and jobs. . . .

The microprocessor will not, then, destroy jobs but transfer them [and the more we plan for this the easier it will be] perhaps from manufacturing to other forms of activity.

Mass unemployment?

Automation will affect the general level of employment, in industries besides those directly affected, through its effects on leakages and injections. It is possible, at worst, that it will lead to mass unemployment.

Technical progress is likely to bring a transfer of income in the economy. Skilled workers may gain at the expense of unskilled, or shareholders may gain instead of wage-earners. If a 'new breed of super-rich' develops, there may be a change in the amounts of consumption and leakages at each level of income. If savings rise, and other leakages do not change, there will be less consumption demand for goods and services throughout the economy.

Injection demand would itself be affected by a change in consumption. A slower rate of growth of consumption would lead to an 'accelerated' fall in investment in conventional machinery and equipment. This also will reduce the demand for the output of producers in the economy.

If these two effects are all that follow, there will be a shift in the levels of both leakages and injections in the economy (see diagram 1). The equilibrium process will lead to a multiplied fall in national income, and as output drops, so also will the demand for labour. If there was previously full employment, there will now be an excess supply of labour, at existing wage rates (diagram 2). 'Mass unemployment' will result.

... or a new age?

The result might be quite different, however. The rest of us need not be worse off as a result of automation. Leakages and injections may be affected in an altogether different way.

The transfer of income to those working on the new technology might increase total spending on consumption — especially if the government encouraged this result by reducing its rates of taxation. The increased investment in new types of capital might far exceed any other changes in demand in the economy. National output would increase as a result, and bring a boom of new job opportunities. The increased demand for labour would end unemployment of the demand-deficiency type, and might even reduce the numbers directly unemployed by the new technology.

Mass unemployment would not result from the transfer from one type of work to another. The only way in which it would result is 'if demand consistently fell below supply' in the general labour market.

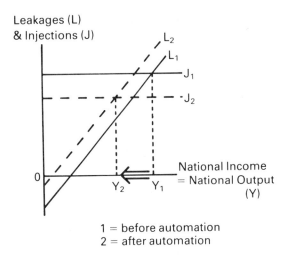

1 = before automation
2 = after automation

Diagram 1   Automation: the effects on output

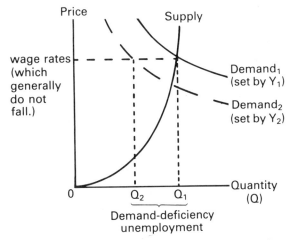

1 = before automation   2 = after automation

Diagram 2   Mass unemployment in the general labour market

QUESTIONS

(i)   Redraw diagrams 1 and 2, on the assumption that consumption and injection demand are both increased by automation.

(ii)   Suggest, in terms of types of leakages and injections, three ways in which the government could provide the extra demand needed to prevent mass unemployment.

(iii)   Draw supply and demand diagrams to show the effects of automation on the market for (a) skilled labour, (b) unskilled labour, directly affected by the change.

4.3 Fiscal policy

Let us assume that the government wishes to end unemployment caused by a general deficiency of demand. In order to do this it will wish to find an appropriate level of output in the economy. Output is set by the levels of leakages and injections, so it is these that the government must aim to influence.

The government will be able to influence each type of leakage in some way, but has most direct control over the level of taxation. This can be changed, in the Budget, as part of *fiscal policy*.

Similarly, the government will be able to influence each type of injection, but can control its own spending most directly. This can be adjusted through fiscal policy, although the government will prefer to decide its level on the basis of long-term, rather than short-term considerations.

The policy method

Fiscal policy will operate through changes in taxation and government spending. The effects of these changes upon both leakages and injections are shown in diagram 1.

If output is too low, at Y_1, there is too little demand to maintain full employment. The amount by which leakages exceed injections at the level of output needed for full employment is shown on the

diagram, and called the *deflationary gap*. A reduction in the rates of taxation would increase the level of consumption demand, as people spent some of their increased disposable income. An increase in the level of government spending would raise injection demand, to the same effect. If the government managed to adjust its budget by exactly the right amount, equilibrium national output would rise to the level needed for full employment at Y_2.

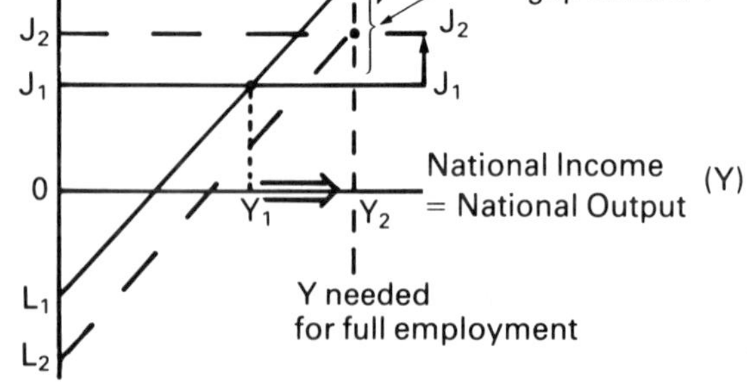

Big deal

Policies to control the economy, in order to limit the level of unemployment, have been in use for many years now. In *Punch*'s satirical account, the policies of Roosevelt, Hitler, and even the Emperor Hadrian, can be seen as public works programmes that reduced the level of unemployment.

In few of these cases, however, can it be claimed that employment policy was the only, or in some cases, the main purpose. As with all government decisions, a wide range of issues will be taken into account, and even if it is agreed how much extra demand is to be generated in the economy, there is still ample room for argument about the best way to do so. By a strange twist of irony, it may be that projects which appear to have no direct connection with employment will be more acceptable to public opinion than others that look too much like aid. The reafforestation of the East End may be a more popular employment policy than Long-Range Strategy Groups.

At what cost?

A policy to expand output and reduce unemployment will require the government to run a budget deficit. Expenditure will need to be more than taxation, or the level of demand in the economy will not respond. This deficit can be financed from the extra leakages that are available in the economy, by borrowing from the savings of the private sector. Borrowing will only be necessary while the unemployment persists, but will need to be repaid at a later date, with interest. This is a direct cost of the policy.

In other ways, there may be additional indirect costs. If the government attempts to fund its deficit by increasing the supply of money in the economy, this may well lead to inflation in later years. (This is considered in chapter 6.) If the government increases demand in the economy by too much, then the money value of national output will increase beyond the level needed for full employment. This will cause an inflationary gap, and prices will rise in

Diagram 1   Fiscal policy to treat a deflationary gap

Big deal

The *Punch* history of how they cut the jobless total

"One of the most ambitious public works programmes ever devised will go before the Cabinet for approval in the autumn if the number of unemployed continues to soar at the present alarming rate."
Sunday Telegraph

(Transcript of a BBC radio programme broadcast on April 1, 1999)

PRESENTER: Good evening. A whole generation has grown up which knows nothing of the excitements and controversies which were roused by Operation Big Deal, the great public works programme initiated by the Government in 1976, in a bold if not frantic attempt to reduce the unemployment figures. In the studio we have a number of survivors of those days and we shall shortly be hearing from them.

As physical reminders of Big Deal we have crumbling stretches of the New Hadrian's Wall built to contain the Scots, a handful of follies on various mountain peaks, a dozen New Forests located in our major cities and a number of office blocks and cut-price country houses built to contain far-fetched departments of State. The Government had hoped to emulate the pump-priming feats of President Roosevelt, with his Tennessee Valley Authority, and Adolf Hitler, who employed armies of unemployed to build the *Autobahnen.*

I want to start our discussion by talking about the reafforestation of the East End of London. Sir Arthur Rinse, I believe you were in charge of that imaginative project?

RINSE: Yes, we had this notorious tract of former dockland, between 50,000 and 60,000 acres in all, which had originally been intended for rehousing Cockneys, or whatever they were called, but it was eventually realised that such a concept was altogether too visionary for the twentieth century....

So we decided the best thing to do was to turn the East End into a National Forest, with nature trails, adventure playgrounds and lakes with marinas. Such a project was labour intensive and required little in the way of scarce materials like bricks. As a result we now have wild boar roaming in Stepney where they had been extinct for centuries.

PRESENTER: What happened to the Cockneys?
RINSE: Who knows? Eaten by boars, I shouldn't wonder.

PRESENTER: Of course the workless middle classes, unsuited to physical labour, were a special problem. Lord Wayleave, can you tell us how work was found for them?

WAYLEAVE: Yes, we had a truly wonderful way with redundant white-collar workers. They were recruited into high-sounding but essentially futile bodies like Long-Range Strategy Groups, Special Projects Boards, Research and Development Centres, Integration Councils, Statistical Analysis and Interpretation Units, Community Relations Surveys, Urban Renewal Appraisal Boards, Central Units for Policy Studies, Resettlement Advisory Bureaux and so on. These bodies were concerned, not with work as you and I know it, but with the contemplation and discussion of work projects. The men who staffed them caught their usual trains from the suburbs and had desks and carpets and secretaries. Some of them had a good idea they were on Government relief, but it did their egos good to pretend otherwise.

---

all parts of the economy. Finally, a rise in national income will increase the levels of all leakages, including imports, and this may put a strain upon the balance of payments.

By contrast, the cost may not be as bad as it seems at first glance. Any change in demand will have a multiplied effect upon the level of output, and hence employment, so that only a small budget deficit may be needed to bring a large fall in unemployment. In this respect, the government is doing no more than 'priming the pump' for the economy. Furthermore, it may be possible to match a budget deficit in one year with a surplus in another year, if the economy fluctuates evenly about a 'normal' level of unemployment. Only if the government uses its control of national output to correct types of unemployment other than that caused by general demand deficiency, might the deficit be expected to become a permanent one.

QUESTIONS

(i)   Draw a leakage and injection diagram to show the effects upon output, and the deflationary gap, of the Big Deal programme, assuming that other things stayed unchanged.

(ii)   Assume that the government increased demand by *more* than was necessary to remove demand-deficiency unemployment. Draw a leakage and injection diagram to show the resulting inflationary gap.

(iii)   Consider the two main influences that set the level of planned investment in the economy. Suggest two policies the government might introduce to raise the level of investment spending, in order to increase national output and employment.

(iv)   How would the effects upon output and employment from increased spending on (a) reafforestation and (b) administrative bodies, be different?

5 The market for money

5.1 What is money?

Free from cares

Many different things have been used as money at various times, in various places. Precious metals, salt, cowrie shells, and most strange of all, pieces of printed paper, have been used in various economic systems. And serving as the local currency, within the closed economy of a Holiday Club, we find coloured beads. What is it that makes beads become money?

Anything that is generally acceptable in the settlement of debt is money. Within the Holiday Club, in exchange for drinks (which are all that can be bought), these beads are completely acceptable.

Money acts as a medium of exchange, and is desired, not for itself, but for the things for which it

---

Free from cares

Life at the Club is free from cares, live in a swimming costume or pareo... and forget about money problems. The price of your holiday includes absolutely everything, except the excursions which depend on your choice. The only other non-inclusive facility is the bar where you can meet for aperitives or after-dinner drinks. To avoid the problems of handling money which is easily lost on the beach or blown away by the wind, the Club has created the Bar necklace. A hostess will give you one against your signature and you can settle the bill at the end of your stay. This multicoloured necklace is your wallet and allows you to buy with 2 black beads, 1 beige bead or 3 golden beads a variety of drinks. Clever and very practical.

---

can be exchanged. It is valued for the potential purchasing power that it represents. These beads are not kept for their beauty, but in order to be rid of them, in exchange for drinks. If they were not acceptable in exchange they would be discarded for being worthless — as perhaps they are, at the end of the holiday.

Money acts as a store of wealth, and as a unit of account. If the exchange value of money is incon-

sistent, it will not be trusted for either of these purposes. Beads will only work well as money so long as there is confidence in them. If people at the Holiday Club refuse to believe that they are of value, then they will not have any value.

Money, income and loans

Money represents the ability to buy goods and services. It can be exchanged for real income, as indeed it is at each stage of the circular flow. To each person who has some money, however, there is a choice to be made, as to how best to use it. Should he spend it himself, or should he lend it to someone else, for them to spend instead?

If he spends the money, he receives in exchange an income of goods and services, that can give real benefits in consumption. If he lends it, he will be giving up those benefits for the duration of the loan. The borrower will have them instead.

Loans can be of different lengths of time, and of different risks, and so they will involve giving up purchasing power to different extents. The amount of purchasing power that is given up in monetary exchange is measured as *liquidity*. Highly liquid loans are, from the lender's point of view, very near to being money, since they can be exchanged for real income, only a little less quickly. The liquidity of loans will set their prices, in the form of the rates of interest that must be paid on them.

Money that is spent is exchanged for real income, but money that is lent is exchanged for a rate of interest, together with the prospect of increased real income in the future.

The liquidity ladder

These two quite different uses of money can be expressed in terms of a 'liquidity ladder'. Money can be exchanged for real goods and services, in the circular flow of income, at ground level. Money can be exchanged in loans of purchasing power, arranged in the monetary markets of the economy, on the ladder itself.

Lenders must climb away from the ability to gain real income, to an extent that is measured by liquidity, and rewarded in the payment of interest. Having made a loan, they will be in possession of an illiquid monetary asset, which will take time to become money once more (the time it takes to climb down the ladder!). In the meantime, they will only be able to obtain their money if they can persuade another to take their place; and it is only by having money that they can obtain, in exchange, real goods and services.

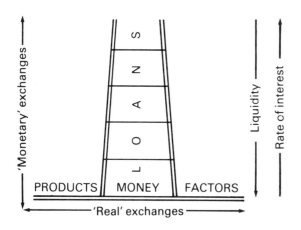

Diagram 1   The liquidity ladder

Interest rates

The liquidity of a loan is set by the amount of purchasing power that is exchanged. This will depend, to an extent, upon the risks involved. It will also depend, heavily, upon the length of the loan. Longer-term loans are less liquid, and accordingly pay a higher rate of interest.

The structure of interest rates, for certain types of loans, is shown in chart 1. The rates of all loans change from time to time, due to changes in the general levels of supply and demand in the monetary markets. The pattern of rates, however, is generally consistent. Longer-term loans pay higher rates of interest. So it is true that 'Time is money'! (diagram 1).

QUESTIONS

(i)   Suggest three reasons why beads would *not* be a suitable form of money for use in a complex, national economy.

(ii)   From chart 1, for July, within which range of interest rates would you expect to find the return on (a) overnight bank loans, (b) government stock with one year to maturity?

(iii)   Suggest one reason why the rate of interest on three-monthly inter-bank deposits should be higher than that on three-monthly Treasury Bills.

(iv)   Explain when, between July and April, the Government Broker should have chosen to sell extra stock, to raise funds for the government.

(v)   How would you have expected the relative amounts of their purchasing potential that people chose to keep in cash and loans to have changed between July and April?

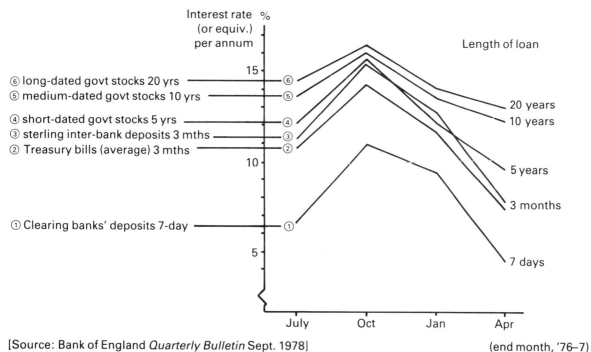

[Source: Bank of England *Quarterly Bulletin* Sept. 1978]   (end month, '76–7)

Chart 1   Interest rates

5.2 The supply of money

Money is generally acceptable in the settlement of debt. Cash is money, since it represents immediate purchasing potential, but certain types of loans are only very slightly less acceptable as money.

Official measures of the supply of money take account of the 'sliding scale' of liquidity. The narrow measure (M1) takes the most acceptable forms of money, kept in notes and coins, and bank current accounts (or 'sight' deposits). The broader measure (M3) includes, in addition, money kept in bank deposit accounts (or 'time' deposits).

The major part of money (M3) is kept in bank accounts. Any explanation of the supply of money, therefore, must explain how banks behave and how they set the amount which they keep 'in their books'.

Banking

The behaviour of banks must be understood in terms of their *liabilities* and *assets*. A bank borrows funds from one source or another, and uses these funds in various ways. A bank's liabilities are the resources it has borrowed, and its assets are the resources it owns.

A bank will usually make use of its funds in two ways. Some it will keep in reserve, to an extent depending upon the particular circumstances of the bank, and use it to cover the withdrawals that are 'liable' to be made from day to day. The remainder it will use to make loans, at a rate of interest, to customers.

A bank that borrows money, and lends money, will only gain from the exchange if it borrows at a lower rate of interest than that at which it lends. Interest rates reflect liquidity, in the way shown by the 'liquidity ladder', and are generally greater for longer-term loans. Liquidity is affected by risk as well, but a guide for profitable banking is often to 'borrow short and lend long'.

The country banker

In the nineteenth century, the business of banking was less complicated, but also less secure, than it is today. There was less variety in the loans made to and from banks, but there was also less confidence shown by depositors in their banks, and funds were more liable to be withdrawn. Both these points are reflected in the assets and liabilities of a small country bank of the 1880s.

One-third of all assets were kept 'in reserve' to cover possible withdrawals of public liabilities. The size of this reserve would have reflected the probable demands upon the bank. If 'the character of the deposits held ... is permanence', a lower reserve would be possible. If it is 'instability', a greater reserve would be necessary. In modern times, a minimum reserve of 12½% is thought sufficient.

The funds borrowed by the country bank could have been withdrawn 'within the compass of a few months'. The loans it has made to others — in the form of 'bills of exchange, advances, and overdrafts, etc.' — were for a much longer period of time. The bank gained a return by lending at a higher rate of interest than that at which it borrowed, but it could, at worst, expect to be bankrupt within a few weeks.

Credit creation

Customers do not borrow from banks and pay a rate of interest, in order to leave that money idle. Loans given out by a bank will be spent, and re-deposited in either the same or another bank. In this way an initial deposit in a bank leads to further deposits, and a *multiplied* increase in the supply of money.

The size of the total increase in money supply that follows any initial increase will depend upon how much of each new deposit is kept in reserve, and how much is lent out for further use. The value of the credit multiplier will be:

$$\frac{100\%}{\% \text{ of assets kept in reserve}}$$

It is through this process of credit creation that banks set the total amount of money in the economy.

Banks and the supply of money

Let us imagine that a local farmer had £100 in gold sovereigns. He had previously hidden them at home, so that they were not in circulation as part of the supply of money. If he now deposited them with our country bank, there would be a chain reaction, causing a multiplied increase in the money supply.

If the bank kept 25% of assets in reserve, ($£100 \times \frac{3}{4} =$) £75 of the new deposit could be lent to other customers, at a rate of interest. If they spent locally, and others received payments which they deposited with the bank, there would be further loans of ($£75 \times \frac{3}{4} =$) £56.25. The process could continue until the total, multiplied increase in the supply of money became ($£100 \times \frac{100\%}{25\%} =$) £400.

The same process works today, within the banking sector as a whole. It explains why most money is in the form of bank accounts; and why the government, if ever it wishes to affect the supply of money, must control the behaviour of banks.

The country banker

See'st thou good dayes? Prepare for evil times: no summer but hath his winter. He never reaped comfort in adversity that sowed it not in prosperity. Quarles.

Let us assume, then, that on your accession to the management-in-chief of the District Union Bank, its Liabilities and Assets are as understated, and that the apportionment of the assets rests on the following basis:–

The Reserve is taken at ONE-THIRD the Liabilities to the public:

The Advances are taken at the amount of Capital and Rest, plus ONE-FIFTH of the liabilities to the public.

The remaining resources of the Bank are absorbed in Bills of Exchange.

These figures are purely arbitrary; but they will serve, as well as others, as a basis for discussion.

And first, as regards the liability side of your position. You are indebted then, to depositors and others, some two and a half millions sterling.

Now, although it is certainly within the range of possibility that you might be called upon, at any time, to redeem the whole of this formidable liability within the compass of a few weeks, the chances are nevertheless as millions to one against such a contingency ever coming to pass.

You will find that, in ordinary times, your deposits, as a whole, maintain a moderately uniform level. The deviations on either side of the main line of average will be slight. A decrease at one point will be met by an increase at another; the closure of some accounts by the opening of fresh ones, and so forth: the general result being that, apart from these slight movements – these ripples on the surface, so to speak – the great volume of your deposits is never stirred to its depths. The minor fluctuations, of which we now speak, are sufficiently provided for by your cash in hand; in fact, this is the primary use of your till-money.

LIABILITIES

On Deposit Receipts	£1,350,000	
On Current Accounts.	.1,050,000	
		2,400,000
Notes in circulation.		50,000
Drafts after date.		20,000
Acceptances by Bank.		30,000
Bills for collection and other items		50,000
Total liabilities to the Public		£2,550,000
Paid-up Capital	£300,000	
Rest, or Surplus Fund	.150,000	
		450,000
		£3,000,000

ASSETS

Reserve:		
Cash in hand.		£200,000
Money at call and short notice . .		350,000
Consols.		300,000
		850,000
Advances, overdrafts, etc.		960,000
Bills of Exchange		1,190,000
		£3,000,000

THE RESERVE. To guard against all probable demands, therefore, I have put your immediately available resources – your financial reserve – at one-third the amount of your liabilities to the public.

This provision will appear to some to be excessive. It is certainly in excess of the reserve usually held by some country banks; whilst it is less than that maintained by others. The range of usage in this matter is very great, and is governed, in some measure, by the character of the deposits held.

In agricultural districts their feature is permanence. In centres of industrial activity, their feature is instability. A ratio of reserve, therefore, which might be more than ample in one case, might be dangerously inadequate in another. Country banks, like yourselves, holding from one to three millions of deposits, hold average reserves of 24 per cent. Others, holding from three to five millions, have reserves averaging 36 per cent. *The Economist,* 19 May, 1883

QUESTIONS

(i) Refer to the accounts of the country bank shown. From whom have the non-public liabilities been borrowed, and for what length of time?

(ii) Arrange the following in order of decreasing liquidity: (a) deposit receipts, (b) current accounts, (c) cash in hand, (d) money at call and short notice, (e) advances, (f) bills of exchange.

(iii) Calculate the value of the credit multiplier for a banking sector with a reserve ratio of (a) 36%, (b) 12½%.

(iv) Imagine that the country bank described in the accounts changes its reserve ratio from one-third to one-quarter of liabilities to the public. Assuming that all the extra loans it supplies are redeposited with it, by how much will the supply of money increase?

5.3 The demand for money

Everyone wants money, in order to be rid of it again, in exchange for real goods and services. This is not a demand for money, but rather for the things money can buy.

To demand money as an end in itself is very different, and apparently the worse of two alternatives. On the one hand, money can be exchanged for goods that give real benefits. On the other hand, it can be lent to someone else to earn a rate of interest. It makes sense, therefore, to spend money or to lend money, but not, at first sight, to hold on to money. Why does a demand to hold money exist?

Cash flow problems

Firms decide to hold cash for reasons that make 'commercial sense'. They must be aware at all times, however, that 'cash is expensive to hold'. Although it may involve no direct cost, it carries an opportunity cost, from the earnings that could be achieved, by

---

Cash flow problems

Cash is both an essential input and a major product of a company's operations. As an input, it is important to know whether the quantity available on given dates is sufficient to meet requirements. A shortage may incur unnecessary costs and involve unnecessary risks. When viewed as a product, the reinvestment problem becomes important. Too much idle cash is a waste of scarce resources. ... A firm may be making a product which outsells its competitors. In addition it may be immensely profitable, but unless its cash is well managed these earnings might never be realised. Many a company has foundered for lack of cash, and the number of technical insolvencies recorded in the financial press is a warning to all financial managers. A far greater number of firms waste a surprising proportion of their resources by holding excessive amounts of cash.

Earnings from cash are zero. Earnings from near cash are, at best, not much more than half that to be obtained in business operations. Consequently, large cash and near cash balances are expensive to hold. None the less, many firms keep sums of cash in hand that far exceed their monthly requirements. When pressed for an explanation some reply that they are saving for a major capital investment. Others state that they can never tell when an investment opportunity will arise or a takeover be proposed. To be prepared they must have a lot of cash in hand. Such arguments may appear to be persuasive but their commercial sense is poor. ... Too much liquidity is a misuse of money. Too little leads to severe cash problems which can result in an inability to be able to settle debts when due.

---

using those funds in 'business operations'. The choice of how to 'reinvest' funds, whether in loans, in equipment, or in cash, is an important one to the firm. 'Too much idle cash is a waste of scarce resources.'

Transactions demand

Not all cash is 'idle', however. Much will be kept for active reasons, because it is intended for spending. Firms are engaged in settling debts of many different kinds from day to day. When buying raw materials, employing labour, hiring capital and land or whatever, they will need to pay cash in exchange. To cover the payments which they expect to be called on to make on a regular basis, firms will keep a balance of cash close to hand. This is a *transactions* demand to hold cash.

If too little cash is kept available, this 'can result in an inability to be able to settle debts when due'. The company may be extremely successful, and possess a large amount of assets, both monetary and real. If, however, it has managed its cash flow badly, it may still be declared 'technically insolvent', and go out of business.

There can also be a *precautionary demand* to hold cash, because purchases *may* have to be made. A private person will carry money in his pocket 'just in case', and a company may keep a lot of cash in hand 'to be prepared'. This also involves keeping cash for active reasons — so that it is available for spending.

Liquidity preference

The reasons that explain the demand to hold cash, will also explain the demand to keep potential purchasing power in liquid, rather than illiquid, form. Just as a bank can keep assets besides cash in its 'liquid reserve', so also can a company keep its purchasing power, close to hand, in liquid assets besides cash. *Liquidity preference* will measure a company's wish to hold cash, and near cash. It will measure, in addition, the desires of lenders to lend on the short, rather than the long-term.

QUESTIONS

(i) How would you expect the transactions and precautionary motives for holding money to be affected by (a) inflation, (b) a rise in interest rates?
(ii) Why is it 'poor commercial sense' to hold cash as 'saving for a major capital investment'?
(iii) What is 'near-cash'? Why does it bring earnings although cash does not?

Speculative demand

Money balances are not always held for active reasons. Under special circumstances, it will be profitable to hold on to money, even though it is not intended for spending, as an act of *speculation*. This will be so, in preference to the two alternative courses of action.

The alternative of spending money 'now' may become unattractive if the prices of goods and services are expected to fall, so allowing even more to be bought in the future. The alternative of lending money at a rate of interest that is fixed 'now' may become unattractive if the rate of interest on offer is expected to be higher in the future.

This leads to a demand to hold money that will often be temporary, and based entirely upon people's expectations. It will, however, offer a third motive for preferring liquid to illiquid assets.

A money market drama

Many influences can affect supply and demand in the market for loans, and so cause a rise in interest rates. If those with funds to supply to the market expect such a change in the future, they will not wish to be committed to long-term loans, on which the rate of interest is fixed at present levels. They will prefer, for the time being, to hold their funds in liquid form.

This response was at work during the first part of the week of 'drama' in the money market. The prospect of government action to raise interest rates meant that 'funds were attracted to the very short periods', instead of to longer-term loans.

From Thursday, expectations changed. Suppliers decided to lend funds for longer-term loans once more, as their liquidity preference fell. They supplied on such a scale that the government could increase their demand for loans, by 'selling the long tap' of long-term stock. Even so, there was a slight fall in the rates of interest set for long-term loans.

The changes in speculative liquidity preference over this week show how temporary, and changeable, this type of demand can be. It follows only people's expectations of future changes which, as in this case, can be wrong. Nevertheless, this causes changes in the whole pattern, and level of interest rates. It does so by influencing demand, in the market for money, and supply, in the market for loans.

A money market drama

The theme of television's next soap opera may yet turn out to be the London money market. What it lacks in human interest it more than makes up for by its drama. A general lack of stability should help the story line, and after going through various changes of mood last week there was even a happy ending to the latest episode.

The mood of the market last week was nervous from the start, building up to panic and chaos on Wednesday morning, but ending on a much better note than could have been expected.

Discount houses did not regard the threat of labour unrest or the rise in the banking systems eligible liabilities without some alarm, but at least it helped to keep the overnight money situation in their favour, as funds were attracted to the very short periods. Longer term rates rose sharply at the same time.

The authorities showed less sign of nerves, however, and seemed content to buy Treasury bills from the houses to relieve any day-to-day shortage. Fears about the money supply and the labour situation led to a marking up of Treasury bill rates on Wednesday morning, pointing towards a small rise in MLR.

News that the miners had voted to accept a settlement within the Government's pay guidelines turned everything round, however, and by Thursday the market was even being philosophical about the money supply. The Government broker took the opportunity to start selling the long tap, something which would have been unthinkable 24 hours earlier, and interest rates declined in calm and easy conditions. By Wednesday evening a rise in MLR was unlikely, and by the close on Thursday was almost out of the question.

Further gilt-edged stock was sold by the authorities on Friday, but on a smaller scale, and money market conditions this week may be influenced by the extent of any further sales. Publication of the trade figures on Tuesday will also be looked at with interest, as well as the money supply and labour situation.

QUESTIONS

(i)   How would you have expected the supply of money (M3) to have changed during the week of 'drama' in the money market?

(ii)   Draw a supply and demand diagram to compare the situations in the market for long-term government stock on (a) Tuesday, (b) Thursday.

(iii)   Explain the effects that you would expect to follow in the money market if *poor* trade figures were to be published on Tuesday.

6 Money, prices and output

6.1 The equation of exchange

The circular flow of income shows that there is a continuing exchange between consumers and producers in the economy. In a complex economy the value of each individual exchange and the total value of all economic activity will both be measured in money terms, as the total amount that producers earn and the total amount that consumers spend. This identity of spending and earning is expressed in the *equation of exchange.*

Spending

In a monetary economy, the total value of spending over a given period of time must be measured in terms of money. The amount of money in the economy (M), and the number of times that each unit of money is spent (the velocity of circulation of money, V) will between them measure the total value of spending (MV).

The supply of money is explained, in the main, by the behaviour of banks. Through the credit creation process, they will expand the amount of money that is kept as book entries, in bank accounts.

The velocity of circulation of money depends exactly upon people's desire to hold on to it. If the demand to hold money balances is very high, money will be spent much less quickly. The demand to hold money is explained by transactions, precautionary and speculative motives, and if those motives set a high level of liquidity preference, the velocity of circulation of money will be low.

Earning

Income is earned by selling goods and services. The total revenue earned from each sale can be found by multiplying the number of units sold by the price of each.

So, at a national level, the general price level (P), and the volume of transactions (T) will between them measure the total level of earnings over a given period of time (PT).

The general price level is usually measured through

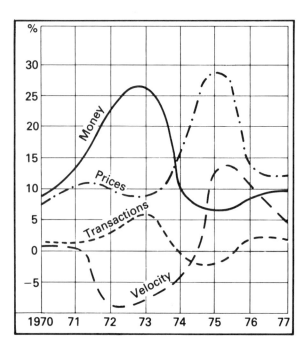

Chart 1   The equation of exchange

a cost of living index. If the index rises, it must be because prices have risen without being offset by falls elsewhere. A rise in the general price level shows that each unit of money can buy only fewer goods and services. This is inflation.

The volume of transactions represents the level of economic activity in the economy. More transactions will imply that there is more real output being produced, and a greater level of real income. Changes in the level of real output will be explained by changes in leakages and injections, and lead to changes in the level of employment of labour, as studied earlier.

MV = PT

The money value of national income can be expressed in terms either of spending or earning. Since the two are always identical, the equation of exchange can be expressed in the form MV = PT. A change in any one of the four components in the equation must then be balanced by changes in one or more of the other components, for the identity to hold.

1970–77

The connections between M, V, P and T over the period from 1970 to 1977 are described in the extract, and in its chart. Since the values are expressed as the percentage change in each, at an annual rate,

1970–77

In the long run there can scarcely fail to be some relationship between money and prices. M V-P T is an identity, in other words it is axiomatic that the stock of money times the velocity of circulation will be equal to prices times the number of transactions. But clearly a change in M can in theory be balanced by a change in V or T just as easily as by a change in P.

What seems to happen in practice is that the first reaction to a reduction in money is an increase in the velocity of circulation followed by a fall in output and only after that a slowing down in prices. When money becomes scarce people hold smaller balances and money moves round faster. A little later lower demand reduces output and as capacity utilisation falls, pressure on prices is reduced.

Chart 1 shows the change in the four variables since the beginning of the decade. During the severe monetary squeeze of 1974 and 1975 velocity rose sharply in the first instance to offset financial scarcity. At the same time inflation was peaking as a result of the monetary expansion two years earlier. Real output has followed the path of money supply closely with a short lag.

Crucial to monetarist theory is that the velocity of circulation should not be infinitely flexible. If that were so there need be no link at all between money supply and prices. This is much the same as saying that there must be a stable demand for money, but despite intense research it has not been easy to establish such a relationship in the United Kingdom. . . .

In open economies like the United Kingdom, where a high proportion of output is internationally traded, the exchange rate may accelerate the effect on prices. With a floating rate, money in excess of demand will tend to flow out of the country to places where there is more demand for it, in other words where a tighter monetary policy is in operation. If no reserves are supplied by the authorities the exchange rate will balance at a lower level and the fall in the pound will rapidly come through to prices. A fixed rate in these circumstances can only be held until the reserves run out. . . . .

I have not dared to confuse the issue with the rather important question of what is money. But as the American economist Kenneth Bolding put it some years ago at a dinner in honour of Milton Friedman:

We must have a good definition of money,
For if we have not, then what have we got?
A Quantity Theory of God knows what.
And that would be almost too true to be funny.

the growth of MV must equal the growth of PT in each year.

In 1970, for instance, there was about a 9% increase in the money supply, and a 1% increase in its velocity of circulation. In total, therefore, the money value of national income grew by 10%. This was matched by a rise in prices of about 7½%, and a rise in the volume of transactions, of about 2½%. Overall, MV equalled PT.

More significantly, the equation of exchange allows us to predict the possible effects of a change in any of the values. In 1974 and 1975, for instance, there was a 'severe monetary squeeze', and 'inflation was peaking'. M grew more slowly, and P rose rapidly. According to MV = PT, this would be associated with a significant rise in the growth of V, or fall in the growth of T. In fact, the growth in real output remained stable, but the growth of the velocity of circulation increased dramatically, from −4% to +13%.

Difficulties

The identity of earning and spending is, therefore, both complete and permanent. This does not tell us, however, which value will *cause* changes in the others: this has yet to be considered. Neither can the various values always be measured as accurately, or as separately, as this example would suggest. We have already seen, for instance, the problems that arise in trying to measure the supply of money.

QUESTIONS

Use the data in chart 1 to answer the following questions.

(i) If the government wished to see inflation fall, and growth to rise, in which years did they succeed in both?

(ii) Estimate in which of the years between 1970 and 1977 (a) liquidity preference decreased, (b) unemployment increased.

(iii) Assume that V and T did *not* change from 1970 to 1977, but that M behaved as shown. What would the change in P have been in (a) 1973 and (b) 1975?

(iv) Assume that the supply of money, in 1977, rose by 20% instead of 10%. According to the connections described in the extract, what would you have expected the levels of V, P and T to have been in that same year?

6.2 The quantity theory

A *monetarist* view of the economy holds that the monetary sector, and the production sector behave quite separately. The levels of supply and demand in the market for money will affect the value of money itself, but not the level of real output.

A *Keynesian* view of the economy is based on a close connection between the different sectors of the economy, where each of the levels of output, employment, and prices is set.

Thus a change in the supply of money will have a different effect from each point of view. Its monetary effect will be to alter the level of prices alone, while in Keynesian terms, it will mainly change real output.

The quantity theory of money

Monetarism is founded on the quantity theory of money, which states that changes in the supply of money will cause proportionate changes in the general level of prices. In terms of the equation of exchange, a change in M will cause an equal change in P. This can only hold if other variables are not affected by the change, and V and T remain untouched.

These two conditions will hold more readily, the longer the period that is taken into consideration. In the long term, liquidity preference will be set by the transactions demand to hold money. The level of output can be assumed to remain close to its full capacity level.

In practice

The effects of changes in the supply of money during much of the 1970s were shown in the last extract. That set out a compromise between the monetarist and Keynesian views.

In the short-term, for a year or two after each change, the Keynesian view seemed to hold. A rise in the supply of money was reflected at first in a fall in the 'velocity of circulation, followed by a fall in output'.

In the long-term, after a delay of two years or so, the monetarist view applied. A rise in money supply brought a matching change in prices, which would be the most significant and enduring of all the changes.

Why does it happen?

Changes in the money supply cause these effects in the following way. If the government allows banks to increase the supply of money, this will at first be absorbed in money balances, as liquidity preference rises. This can only be for speculative reasons, as

potential lenders wait for the rates of interest on long-term loans to return to reasonably high levels.

With more purchasing potential in their hands, people will then begin to spend money on consumption goods (in a monetarist view) or lend it to others to spend on investment goods (in a Keynesian view). The increased demand for goods at first will raise real output. As full capacity is reached in each industry, prices will then begin to rise. In this way, money sets prices.

Policy intentions

A rise in the supply of money seems to raise real output, and hence employment, in the short-term, but to cause inflation in the long-term. If the government wishes to control inflation, it must control the supply of money. This is a basis for the government's monetary policy.

Although the money supply is to be set to grow at a pace that will not cause inflation, this does not mean that it must not grow at all. Real output will expand in most years, due to improvements in productivity, and a certain rate of inflation may have to be accepted as unavoidable. Between them, these rates of growth will need to be matched by growth in the supply of money, according to MV = PT.

Control of the money supply is a long-term policy — its effects on prices will only be seen after two years, or so. Unexpected and sudden changes in liquidity preference, in the rate of inflation, or in the growth of output cannot be accommodated in this policy. This can lead to difficulty.

Lorry drivers' test run

If the government maintains strict controls on the rate of growth of purchasing power, then, in terms of the equation of exchange, MV should grow at a steady and predetermined rate. This is the situation that is described in the extract.

Changes in the economy must therefore be absorbed within the money value of national output, for PT will only be able to expand at the same rate as MV. An extra rise in prices — from import prices, or wage costs, or whatever — must result in a lower rise in output, and vice versa. If excessive wage settlements bring increased price rises, then the level of real output can only rise by less.

Let us suppose that, at the time of the lorry drivers' wage settlement, money supply was increasing by 10% a year, and that its velocity of circulation did not change. MV was rising, therefore, by 10%, and PT could also rise by only the same rate. A pay increase to lorry drivers of 15% would be likely to lead to

Lorry drivers' test run . . .

Whatever other significance the present trial by trade union may ultimately have for the nation it should provide a good test of monetarism. For almost the first time in recent British history strong wage pressure is developing while the Government keeps expansion in the money supply under firm control.

According to the monetarists if the Government sticks to its guns and declines to finance the higher settlements by printing more money then pay increases cannot lead to price increases, except perhaps to a limited extent for a limited period.

This was not the case in 1974 and 1975 when pay and subsequently prices rose very rapidly while the money supply expanded by only 10 p.c. followed by 6½ p.c. But it has always been possible to argue that the price explosion of 1975 reflected the monetary expansion under the Conservatives of 2-3 years earlier. This time the monetary squeeze starts from a position closer to equilibrium.

In the middle of the current industrial turmoil with the lorry-drivers likely to settle for over 15 p.c. it is difficult to believe with monetary fundamentalists that average pay increases cannot be pushed up, at any rate for a time, by organised labour irrespective of monetary discipline.

There are already signs, for instance that the supply of money is being made to work harder and the velocity of circulation is going up. While the economy continued to grow and inflation levelled off in the second half of last year monetary expansion slowed down implying higher velocity.

Later, high pay settlements are likely to price workers out of jobs. Whether the increase in industry's costs comes through to prices depends on the productivity of the workers remaining. At any rate a tight monetary policy should at least restrain the transfer of pay increases to prices by keeping the pound higher than it would otherwise have been. The foreign exchange and gilt-edged markets, though not immune from the national despondency, have not been panic selling in the traditional manner.

Pay policies in theory help to stop workers pricing themselves, and others, out of jobs. But in practice they have introduced such distortions in pay levels that they have contributed to their own destruction.

similar increases for other groups of workers, and to similar increases in the prices of the goods and services they produce. If prices were to rise by 15% and PT only by 10%, real output would inevitably *fall* by 5%.

In this way, 'high pay settlements are likely to price workers out of jobs'. The pressure, or the risk, of this unemployment would presumably affect the demands of trade unions. If so, 'then pay increases cannot lead to price increases, except perhaps to a limited extent for a limited period'. In the short-term there might be changes in the level of real output, and the level of employment. In the long-term, the quantity theory would apply, and price rises would be set by the growth of money supply alone.

QUESTIONS

(i) Explain the 'higher velocity . . . in the second half of last year', that is described in the extract.

(ii) From the data in the previous extract, what would you have expected the rate of inflation to have been in (a) 1978, (b) 1979?

(iii) How might a pay increase to lorry drivers of 15% lead to an increase in T *rather* than P?

(iv) Draw a leakage and injection diagram to show, in Keynesian terms, how an increase in the supply of money will cause a rise in the money value of national output.

6.3 Monetary policy

Monetarist theory shows that the quantity of money in an economy will affect the general level of prices. Keynesian theory shows that interest rates affect the level of investment, money, national output, and employment. Governments are concerned about all of these effects, and will therefore need monetary policies to control both the money supply and interest rates.

At any one time, there are many different types of money, and near-money, and many different levels of interest rates. An effective monetary policy will therefore need several weapons in its armoury in order to be able to attack all these different targets. The details of the ground where the fight is joined and of the techniques for using the weapons, will not be considered here. We will try merely to set down the general principles which fashion the policy.

The supply of money, and the prices of loans are both explained by the behaviour of banks, in the various monetary markets. The work of controlling that behaviour for the purposes of monetary policy, is taken on by the Bank of England, acting on behalf of the government. The Bank of England has a full working relationship with all the other banks in the monetary world, and it is this daily contact that provides the opportunities for controlling money and interest rates. What are these opportunities?

The Bank of England

One way to approach the work of the Bank of England is through the accounts of its Banking Department, which are published regularly in its *Quarterly Bulletin*. The particular value of each entry in the accounts need take very little of our interest here, but the headings in the accounts will signify the main points of contact between the Bank of England and the rest of the banking community (see table 1).

Bankers' deposits

All banks have to keep a current account at the Bank of England. Although the size of this account is laid down for them, they find it useful in their daily work of balancing debts with each other, by transferring funds from one account to another. Since this money belongs to the banks, and is deposited as a loan, it is, from the Bank of England's point of view, a liability that could be withdrawn.

Should the Bank of England wish to reduce the supply of money, it now has an opportunity to do so. Large sums are under its own, direct control, and can be 'claimed' temporarily. Money that is transferred into 'special deposits' in this way is still owned by other banks, but is no longer available to them for use as part of their reserves. As shown in an earlier section (see page 28), this will lead to a multiplied reduction in their lending, and a fall in the supply of money.

Government securities

As part of its function as banker to the government, the Bank of England is responsible for raising loans made to the government in the monetary markets. For the most part this is achieved by selling government securities on the open market, and Treasury Bills to the discount market. The main concern will always be to raise as much money as the government wishes to borrow, and to do so at as little cost as possible. But, in addition, these *open-market operations* provide a second opportunity for monetary policy.

By selling, for instance, more securities, the authorities change the conditions of supply in the market, and encourage a fall in price. Investors receive fixed annual payments from their ownership of stocks, which they can now obtain at lower cost. The return on investment, and effective rate of interest, has risen. At the same time, investors reduce their money balances to buy the securities and, providing the extra money borrowed by the government is not respent, the supply of money falls.

In this way, the Bank of England can use its position as a price-setter in the market for loans to affect the supply of money, the general pattern of loans, and rates of interest.

Advances

As part of its special relationship with the discount houses, the Bank of England will always lend to them as a last resort. The rate at which it will lend on such occasions is called its *Minimum Lending Rate*. In order to ensure that it is only used as a last resort, this rate is set slightly above that at which the discount houses themselves lend money, when buying Treasury Bills.

Changes in Minimum Lending Rate will cause a variety of effects in the monetary markets, but the most direct of these will be that felt by discount houses as last resort borrowers. The nature of their business is such that, by borrowing 'at call', and lending for several months, they are subject to very sudden shortages of funds.

They need to borrow from the Bank of England, therefore, often and on a large scale. If the rate at which they will have to borrow is seen to rise, then,

Table 1

Bank of England

£ millions

		Liabilities					Assets			
		Total	Public deposits	Special deposits	Bankers' deposits	Reserves and other accounts	Government securities	Advances and other accounts	Premises, equipment and other securities	Notes and coin
1979	Jan. 17	2.229	25	1.113	405	672	1.789	207	209	24
	Feb. 21	1.343	25	255	404	644	951	212	173	7
	Mar. 21	1.051	28	2	426	580	155	583	298	15
	Apr. 18	1.014	31	—	355	614	608	229	168	9
	May 16	1.919	29	719	559	597	1.535	159	216	9

Banking Department (header above Liabilities/Assets)

From the additional notes to the table:

Banking Department
Through this department the Bank acts as banker to the Government, to the banks, to overseas central banks and international organisations, and to a small number of other domestic institutions and private individuals including staff.

Liabilities
Bankers' deposits are the current accounts held at the Bank by the banks and discount houses.

Assets
Government securities include government and government-guaranteed securities, valued at cost less provision for losses, and Treasury bills.

Advances and other accounts include market advances to the discount market, loans to customers and support loans to deposit-taking institutions. Provisions for losses are deducted.

Source: *Bank of England Quarterly Bulletin* Vol 19, No 2, June 1979

---

to avoid unnecessary losses in the future, they will also need to increase the rates at which they lend.

This third opportunity also allows the Bank of England to influence both the supply of money and the level of interest rates. By being less prepared to lend, and by setting its Minimum Lending Rate at a higher level, it can restrict the supply of money and raise interest rates. By lending more, at a lower rate, it can expand the supply of money and lower interest rates.

Banker to the banks

A fourth opportunity for monetary policy, and the last we will consider here, arises out of the Bank of England's function as banker to the banks. Among the many other connections arising from this every-day work, this requires the Bank of England to offer information and advice to the banking community.

It is a natural next step for them to include with their advice, from time to time, requests that the banks might assist the government in matters of monetary policy. These may take the form of requests, to give priority in lending to industry rather than for private consumption, or to restrict the over-all amount of new lending. Such requests are usually considered favourably by the banks, and not only because of the arsenal of weapons that the Bank of England could introduce to make their point more forcibly.

QUESTIONS

(i) In which two months in the period from January to May 1979 were the authorities most concerned to restrict the supply of money? Explain your answer.

(ii) Draw a supply and demand diagram of the market for government securities, to show the effect of open-market operations intended to lower interest rates.

(iii) Explain how the Bank of England might use open-market operations to make the pattern of liquidity more long-term, without changing the over-all amount of loans.

(iv) Draw a supply and demand diagram of the market for Treasury Bills, to show the effect of an earlier rise in the Bank of England's Minimum Lending Rate.

(v) Explain how a rise in Minimum Lending Rate will affect (a) investment, (b) inflation.

7 Inflation

7.1 Demand inflation

Inflation is a rise in the general price level, and a fall in the value of money in exchange for real goods and services. Inflation tends to continue as a 'spiral', around the circular flow of money income. Higher prices bring higher incomes, which lead to yet higher prices, and yet higher incomes. Once under way, the spiral is very difficult to break, as people's expectations of inflation tend to perpetuate, and even accelerate, it.

The original causes of inflationary pressure can be seen in terms of changes in the conditions of demand or supply, throughout the economy.

Demand inflation and output

An increase in demand for products will encourage rises both in their prices *and* their output. Thus, demand inflation is closely associated with a growth in output, and full employment of factors, throughout the economy. This connection can be seen in terms of the change in the conditions of demand in each market, that will raise prices, and output, as there is a response from suppliers (see diagram 1).

There is some dispute amongst economists over how much prices and output will each respond. Keynesians assert that output, measured in real terms, will adjust first and foremost. This will mean that inflation can only result when the economy is at full capacity, can produce no more real output, and yet continues to face a rise in demand. As a last resort the general price level will rise.

Monetarists hold that a rise in demand throughout the economy (which can be due only to a rise in money supply) will have its main and enduring effect upon prices. Any change in output will occur only in passing, and to a limited extent.

In practice, demand will usually affect both output and prices, to different extents, at different times.

Causes of demand inflation

An increase in demand is seen by Keynesians in terms of leakages and injections.

An *inflationary gap* results when the economy is producing at full capacity, and yet, at that level of output, injections still exceed leakages. In other words, demand from spending on consumption and injections, is greater than the real output that can be supplied by the economy. As the equilibrium process continues, the money value of national income will rise, to the level at which injections match leakages. The change in money values that results from this pressure is an inflation of the general price level (see diagram 2).

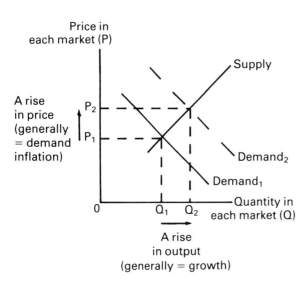

Diagram 1   Demand inflation

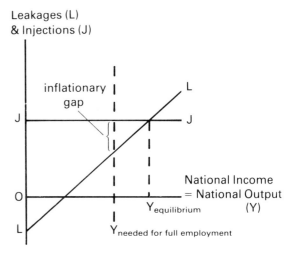

Diagram 2   An inflationary gap

After the slump, look out for the boom

The world recession is now yesterday's worry. Today, the principal anxiety of treasury officials around the world is that demand will rev up so fast this year that another commodity price explosion, like that which sent us all into an inflationary spin in 1973, will occur. . . .

Many of the signs indicate that the world is indeed in a position remarkably similar to that of four years ago, when the recession was ending. The main difference is that prices are much higher now than they were then. Prices of more commodities in world trade, in particular, rose far more in 1973 and 1974 than since the war, and fell last year more sharply than in the previous recession.

This is not in any way due to the fall in sterling. The inflation this article is concerned about is the world-wide one, which tends to form the floor on top of which our (currently) bigger one is built. . . .

Industrial production is rising sharply, especially in the US, Japan, and Germany – which together account for 61% of the output of the developed

(OECD) world. These countries are leading the recovery. . . .

All the major countries – including even Britain – are performing more powerfully so far this year than was expected. The OECD Secretariat has had to revise upwards all its forecasts published in its December Economic Outlook. The average increase for the industrial nations as a group will come out this year at more like 5% than the 4% published.

Japan is not growing as fast as in 1972 – forecasts range between 4.3% and 5.5%, compared with nearly 10% in 1972. The dangers lie mainly in the present rapid rates of recovery in the US and West Germany being sustained for too long. It is good that these countries have taken the lead in pulling the world out of the pit of recession and high unemployment, but stabilisation is a two-way business and a bit of reining back will be needed soon.

Nowhere does there seem to be a strong case for really hard, economic braking. There is a need, though, for some gentle restraining action, early, especially in the US.

. . . it is important to avoid another disaster like the 1973 commodity price explosion.

The inflationary gap results because injections are 'too high' and leakages are 'too low'. The blame for this might fall upon any of the leakages – savings, taxation, or imports – or any of the injections – investment, government spending, or exports. The cure will be to adjust the level of the particular culprit, or any other of the leakages and injections.

After the slump, look out for the boom

The world economy often suffers from fluctuations of demand, and output. For a period of a few years, demand might remain low, but then begin to increase in all countries together. As it does so, world production will rise, and then, as more and more parts of the world economy approach full capacity, demand inflation will occur.

This is the situation that seemed to apply in 1972 and 1973, for instance, when there were excessive increases in demand throughout the world. These caused output to expand greatly, but brought in addition 'a commodity price explosion' and 'an inflationary spin'.

In both the boom of 1972 and 1973, and the 'remarkably similar position now', there has been a close connection between output and prices. In a demand-based boom, both are affected in the same direction, although the order of events seems to follow the 'Keynesian' prescription given earlier. Out-

put rises first, as the economy moves 'out of the pit of recession and high unemployment'. Only if the process continues too far, beyond the level of full capacity output, will inflation result. In other words, the 'dangers lie mainly in the . . . recovery . . . being sustained for too long'.

QUESTIONS

(i)   Suggest reasons why a world commodity 'price explosion' might be described as a 'disaster'.

(ii)   How would you explain the 'present' risk of another world 'inflationary spin' in monetary terms?

(iii)   Suggest three ways in which the governments of the USA and West Germany mght 'rein back'.

(iv)   Draw a leakage and injection diagram to explain 'recession and high unemployment' in the world economy.

7.2 Cost inflation

Attack on inflation

In 1975 the British government launched a new policy to control inflation. It was important for the success of that policy that people believed inflation should be controlled, even at the cost of personal 'sacrifices'. The government could point to many disadvantages from inflation, but concentrated, in the main, upon its effects on output and employment.

We have seen how demand inflation, growth of output, and full employment, all tend to go hand in hand. Here, the government were predicting that inflation would lead to 'firms closing down', and would 'greatly increase unemployment'. This is a direct contradiction of what we would expect. How can it be explained?

Cost inflation and output

The government clearly felt that inflation in 1975 was not caused by changes in demand. The main culprits were described as 'the steep increase in world costs of food and raw materials', and 'big increases in wages'. These would change the conditions of supply in all markets, and cause *cost inflation*.

The shift of supply in each market would be associated with a move along the demand curve, as shown in diagram 1. Firms throughout the economy would tend to raise their prices, and close down some of their lines of production. Cost-based inflation was associated with decreasing output, rising unemployment and 'slump'.

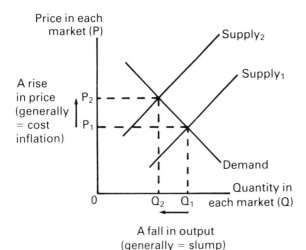

Diagram 1   Cost inflation

Attack on inflation: a policy for survival

The sacrifices called for will not be easy. This will be particularly true in the early months of the policy because of the price increases already in the pipeline. But the alternative is much worse: a continuation of present rates of inflation would –

> greatly increase unemployment
>
> threaten us with external bankruptcy, and
>
> gravely damage the social and economic fabric of the nation.

To try to cure inflation by deliberately creating mass unemployment would cause widespread misery, industrial strife and a total degeneration of our productive capacity.

(From the White Paper,
The Attack on Inflation, Cmnd 6151)

That is the heart of the matter. It is the basis of the Government's policy as announced in the White Paper, *The Attack on Inflation*.

Inflation means more than wages chasing prices and prices chasing wages in an ever more ruinous circle of rising costs and wage packets that buy less and less.

Inflation, if not brought under control, means industrial collapse and national bankruptcy.

At home, it means firms closing down because soaring costs would make it impossible for them to survive. It means jobs lost on a terrifying scale. Lost not only for a few months, but for ever.

Abroad, it means our creditors turning off the taps. It means loss of confidence in the £, and in Britain's ability to recover. It means the destruction of our ability to buy from abroad the materials and goods we need to keep industry going.

So more factories and offices would close down. Many more jobs would be lost. Lost for ever.

Unemployment is already very serious, and growing. The attack on inflation is the essential way to check the rise in unemployment and to avert the threat of millions indefinitely out of work, and young people unable to start their working lives. It offers the best hope of restoring job security and fighting our way back to full employment. . . .

Who is to blame for inflation?
No reasonable person can put all the blame for run-away inflation on wage rises or the trade unions. There are many other causes. There was the steep increase in 1972/73 in world costs of food and raw materials, and the colossal rise in oil prices in 1973/74.

This, of course, hit other countries as well as Britain. But increasingly over the past few months, big increases in wages have pushed up our rate of inflation.

The fact is, other countries have brought down their rate of inflation. We have not.

A policy for survival

As if this was not bad enough, the 1975 inflation brought other disadvantages as well. In the government's view, it was promising to 'threaten us with external bankruptcy', and to 'gravely damage the social and economic fabric of the nation'. These referred in particular to the effects that inflation could have upon the balance of payments, the distribution of income, and the level of capital investment in the economy.

The balance of payments would be affected by a change in the prices of British goods, compared with those in other countries. If inflation 'hit other countries as well as Britain', then prices in all countries would do no more than rise together. If, however, 'other countries have brought down their rate of inflation, we have not', then the long-term result could be for the loss of competitiveness to cause a payments deficit.

If inflation were to affect all prices, costs and incomes equally, there need be no effect upon the distribution of incomes, or the level of capital investment. Not all incomes, however, can rise in line with prices, and those living on 'fixed' incomes tend to suffer. In this way, inflation could cause social hardship.

Similarly, a rise in interest rates in line with rises in other prices, would not cause changes in the process of investment. It is only because investors become uncertain over future prospects, and because savers are less willing to commit themselves to long-term lending, that capital investment is reduced. In time, this would damage the 'economic fabric of the nation', and if it was reflected in an unwillingness from foreigners to lend to Britain, in 'our creditors turning off the taps'.

Causes of cost inflation

Changes in the conditions of supply are part of the normal behaviour of markets, and only in special circumstances will they lead to a general attack of cost inflation. In 1975 the government believed that those circumstances applied.

The rise in the prices of food, raw materials, and oil, throughout the world would have increased the costs of firms which bought them. For this to explain the start of a continuing spiral of price and cost increases, however, two conditions must have been met. One was that any rise in costs was not absorbed by an equal reduction in other costs of production. It could be possible, after all, for either workers, management, or shareholders in each firm to accept a drop in their pay to balance these rises in costs.

The other possibility is that firms could find alternative methods of production which would allow them to reduce their consumption of more costly imports. Unfortunately, the nature of the imports makes this seem unlikely, since the demand for food, raw materials, and oil is highly inelastic with respect to price. Almost the same quantity of each will be bought, despite the rise in their price.

Once the inflation process has begun, it can then be continued, or even exaggerated, by 'big increases in wages'. The ability of labour to maintain this pressure must, again, depend on certain conditions being met, for the pay settlements which are decided must anticipate future rises in the cost of living and so continue the spiral.

The implications for policy are self-evident. The government must try to restrain the cost increases that set the inflation process under way. In some cases, where the cause is found in world demand or supply conditions, these may be beyond their control. Once the inflationary spiral is established, the government must seek to undermine the expectation of future changes, which feeds it. It was for this reason, indeed, that the government published the contents of their 'Attack on Inflation'.

QUESTIONS

(i)   Suggest reasons why inflation might mean that jobs are 'lost not only for a few months, but for ever'.
(ii)   In what sense can inflation lead to 'national bankruptcy'?
(iii)   Explain why a rise in the price of crude oil is more inflationary than a rise in the price of olive oil.
(iv)   Assuming that the supply of money throughout the world stays constant, what would you expect to be the effect of a rise in oil prices, in terms of $MV = PT$?
(v)   Explain why 'curing inflation' might involve 'deliberately creating mass unemployment'.

7.3 Inflation policy

It is very difficult for the government ever to win. There are so many different targets for them to aim at with their economic policy, that, by the laws of chance alone, they are unlikely to be achieving all of them, all of the time. To make matters worse, they have only limited weapons available with which to attack each target. To make matters impossible, many of the targets are closely related, so that as one becomes closer, another moves further away.

Conflict between objectives

All other things being equal, the government will aim to keep the level of unemployment as low as possible, and the growth of output as high as possible. Each of these aims tends to be achieved, however, at the cost of demand-based inflation, a worsening of the balance of payments, and downward pressure on the exchange rate.

A reduction in the rate of inflation, and improvement in both the balance of payments and exchange rate, can often be achieved by demand-deflationary policies. These, however, tend to cause mass unemployment, and low growth of output.

Often, therefore, the government will have to set its priorities between *alternative* targets, or find a compromise which leaves all of them, to some extent, unsatisfied. If the economy is suffering from cost-based inflation, the choice can become even less satisfactory, for cost inflation tends to be associated with a failure to meet *all* the remaining policy goals.

The government can then find itself 'between the devil and the deep blue sea'. Either the economy will suffer from inflation, unemployment, low growth, and external payments and exchange rate difficulties; or, the government can introduce a policy to control inflation, but, in so doing, cause even more unemployment, and even lower growth! This was the choice faced by the government in the last extract, in introducing their 'Attack on Inflation'.

If only Denis *did* know some simple sums

The Chancellor of the Exchequer is responsible for the economic policy of the British government. When there is inflation, of whichever type, he introduces the policies intended to control it. If the policies do not work, or if the government increases inflation by its own actions, he will receive the blame!

Denis Healey was Chancellor of the Exchequer in 1978 when he was blamed for the rate of inflation, and the unpleasant policies he introduced to control it. How fair was this criticism?

Causes of the inflation

It appeared in 1978 as if there were several different causes of the inflation at that time. Possible cost causes were the 'wage explosion', and the decline of the exchange rate. Possible demand causes were the 'vast extra expenditure by the Government', and the 'wave of new money'. The government believed that a large part of the problem was due to excessive rises in wages, and was considering policies to control them. Critics of the government, by contrast, believed that demand causes were to blame, and that these were a direct result of the Chancellor's 'inability to get his sums right'.

As with any inflationary spiral, it is very difficult to discover the cause that first started the cycle of price and cost increases. The wage explosion, for instance, might have been the *starting* point, by increasing the costs of firms, and the incomes of consumers. Alternatively, the same rise in wages might only have *followed* an earlier rise in demand

---

If only Denis *did* know some simple sums

Mr Denis Healey tells us in his entry for Who's Who that he has a first-class degree from Oxford.

It should come as no surprise to anyone that the studies of the younger Healey at Oxford at no point included arithmetic — the subject whose laws he quaintly claimed to be expounding at the weekend.

If there is another wage explosion, he says, he will not hesitate to cut Government spending or raise taxes, or both. That is not a threat, he maintains, merely a description of the laws of arithmetic. . . .

But it should be stated at the outset that the biggest arithmetical problem confronting the nation at large is Mr Healey's consistent inability to get his sums right. . . .

The nation at the moment is trying to deal with two separate difficulties. The first, the rapid rise in wages, is a consequence of miscalculation Mr Healey made in his 1977 Budget strategy.

Theory

And the second, the current size of the Government deficit, arises from miscalculation in Mr Healey's 1978 Budget strategy.

What went wrong in 1977 was that Mr Healey planned to keep down the exchange rate for the pound. (The theory was that this helped exports.)

This involved, for technical reasons, vast extra expenditure by the Government, with the result that the money supply figures went all to pot.

The money supply in the last financial year was

for products, and for the services of factors of production. The starting point for inflation will then have been the rise in demand caused by government spending, in particular, or a rise in money supply, more generally, in the way the critics claimed.

If the initial cause were to be the fault of government, it would almost certainly be as a result of a conflict of objectives. An increase in government spending may be inflationary, but it will tend to lower the level of unemployment and raise the level of output. The rise in the money supply may do the same, but be due, in addition, to a concern to keep the exchange rate of the pound at a competitive level for exports, in order to strengthen the balance of payments and the long-term growth of the economy.

Inflation policy

Fiscal policy can be used to control the overall level of demand in the economy. A reduction in government spending will cut injections, an increase in rates of taxation will raise leakages. Both will tend to reduce national income, and close an 'inflationary gap' in the economy. Even when the inflation is cost-based, then, at the risk of even greater unemployment, these policies will reduce the excess of demand, at current price levels, in all markets.

It is for this reason that Mr Healey predicted that he would possibly 'cut government spending or raise taxes, or both', in order to control wage-push inflation.

Monetary policy can be used in either a Keynesian or a monetarist way. A rise in interest rates might serve to reduce investment, and so close an inflationary gap. This might also limit the growth of the money supply, so that, in terms of the quantity theory of money, there is less long-term pressure on prices. The 'rise in interest rates' introduced by Mr Healey will have been for both of these reasons, but in particular to restrict the growth of the money supply to its 13% target.

Other policies may be appropriate in the face of particular inflationary pressures. A rise in the exchange rate, for instance, will tend to cancel the effect of rising import prices. Special subsidies may ease the impact of sudden cost increases.

There may, finally, be some policies which the government can introduce to moderate the expectations that perpetuate the inflationary spiral. *Prices and incomes policy* is intended to do just this, and the emphasis that was laid upon extreme wage rises by Mr Healey may have been part of this type of strategy.

---

supposed to rise by between 9 per cent and 13 per cent. In fact, it went up 16 per cent.

Both the target and the outcome were far, far too high and it is this wave of new money which is now producing what some would call a wage explosion.

Note an important fact: the money is already there. It is already surging through the economy. There is no way Mr Healey or anyone else can stop it producing a rise in wages (the cost of labour) or a rise in prices (the cost of goods). . . .

On the contrary, the rise in interest rates now has nothing to do with the current round of wage rises. It is, in fact, an attempt to clear up a problem caused by Mr Healey's 1978 Budget.

It became apparent in the last few weeks that the Chancellor was in danger of having a larger Budget deficit than he had planned for; and that he was not going to be able to borrow enough to cover a respectable portion of that deficit.

That, and not any moonshine about wages policy, is why he 'exploded' interest rates and that is why thunder-struck householders up and down the country are staring at an 'explosion' in mortgage rates. . . .

His last Budget cut taxes. It was hinted at briefly that there would be a July Budget with further concessions. Now the prospect is not of a tax-cutting mini-Budget but possibly one which will cut public expenditure or increase taxes or both.

These oscillations, quite frankly, are becoming intolerable. For businessmen in particular.

The sooner the great arithmetician gives way to someone who can, at least, see his way to the end of the month, the better.

QUESTIONS

(i)   Draw a supply and demand diagram of the market for fixed-interest government securities, and use it to help to explain why the 1978 Budget caused a rise in interest rates.

(ii)   Draw a leakage and injection diagram to show the effect of 'the last Budget' on the level of money national income.

(iii)   Under what circumstances would 'the last Budget' have led to demand-inflation?

(iv)   Why is a 'cut in government spending and a rise in taxation' so unpleasant as to be seen as a 'threat'?

(v)   Explain why 'oscillations' in Budget policy should be thought intolerable by investors in business.

Suggested answers

2.1 Away from it all? (i) Real income falls at first, then recovers. (ii) Money income increases. Real income may increase, but mainly changes with types of goods. (iii) Lower money income; different valuation of types of goods received as real income.
High wages (i) Landlord (a) 'rents' out land, (b) keeps a 'plentiful table'; labourer (a) is 'employed in husbandry', (b) 'buys new clothes'. (ii) Money income in higher prices; real income also, if all live 'more plentifully'.

2.2 Disarmament (i) (a) 0.55; (b) 0.7. (ii) Diagram 1. (iii) Incomes greater in the USA. (iv) C = £17 602 million; S = £2272 million. (v) Less consumption of durable goods; S shifts up at each level of income.
World . . trouble (i) 0.19. (ii) Less saving, less spending on imports. (iii) $\frac{1}{6}$. (iv) Decrease in marginal propensities to save/tax/import. (v) A fall of $(\frac{1}{1-\frac{1}{4}} \times £2500m =) £3333$ million.

2.3 Investing (i) Present profit is a source of funds and so affects costs. Prospective profit refers to returns. (ii) Replacement; improvement. (iii) Any change in consumption affects investment in an 'accelerated' way. (iv) Reduce costs by cheap loans, etc.; increase returns by crop price guarantees, etc. (v) Interest rates affect cost; consumption growth and expectations affect returns.

3.1 Revival in output (i) Diagram 2. (ii) Diagram 2. (iii) Savings: HP restrictions, etc.; investment: previous rise in savings; interest rates, etc.
Coffee boom (i) Taxation (leakage) rises; spending (injection) unchanged; budget surplus. (ii) (a) Less savings; more investment; (b) higher world prices; higher taxation; lower government spending. (iii) $(\frac{1}{1-\frac{3}{4}} \times £77m =) £308$ million. (iv) If MPL = 1, MPC = 0. (v) As diagram 4, section 3.1, except that injections *fall* (e.g. 1977 to 1976).

3.2 Does it pay? (i) (a) The valuation of produce consumed at home; (b) produce stored for future planting, etc.; (c) sale of surplus to outside world; (d) all goods bought from outside world. (ii) Value of produce, minus expenditure on inputs. (iii) (a) Not offering all shop services; (b) only after costs of inputs have been subtracted. (iv) When processing fresh food. (v) Less drugs; less driving to shops.

4.1 Future . . jobs (i) Frictional: no change; structural and technological: perhaps increasing despite policies; demand deficiency: unemployment falling. (ii) More supply, less demand in the labour market; diagram 3, 1 to 2; more unemployment at P1, due to excess supply of labour. (iii) Frictional: more information on jobs; structural: grants for geographical mobility; technological: grants for retraining; demand-deficiency: reduce general taxation etc.

4.2 Automation (i) Diagrams 1 and 2, section 4.2, but from 2 to 1. (ii) More I, G, X; less S, T, M. (iii) Diagram 2, section 4.2 (a) from 2 to 1; (b) from 1 to 2.

4.3 Big deal (i) Diagram 1, section 4.3, but a rise in injections only. (ii) Diagram 2, section 7.1. (iii) Lower interest rates, by borrowing less itself; improve expectations; give tax relief on investment returns. (iv) Different types of products; different groups benefit directly; different multiplier effects if MPC of each group is different.

5.1 Money and loans (i) Not sufficiently divisible, convenient, limited in supply, or homogeneous. (ii) (a) 0-6%; (b) 11¼-12% approx. (iii) Loans to the government are less risky. (iv) April, when the cost to the government is least. (v) Into loans in October; into cash in April; (to some extent).

5.2 The country banker (i) Shareholders, and itself; for ever. (ii) (c) (b) (d) (a) (f) (e). (iii) (a) 2.8; (b) 8. (iv) Extra lending is $(\frac{1}{3} - \frac{1}{4}) \times £2\,550\,000$). Multiplier is $(\frac{1}{\frac{1}{4}})$. Total increase, therefore, is $(£212\,600 \times 4 =) £850\,400$.

5.3 Cash flow problems (i) (a) Both increase; (b) precautionary falls. (ii) Savings can be lent, at a rate of interest. (iii) Short-term loans: deposit accounts, etc. They earn a rate of interest.

Money market drama (i) Increase till Thursday, then

fall. (ii) Diagram 4; price of stock rises, real rate of interest falls. (iii) In expectation of government policy to raise interest rates, effects would be as 'before Thursday'.

6.1 1970-77 (i) 1973; 1976. (ii) (a) 1970; 1975; 1976; 1977; (b) 1974; 1975. (iii) (a) 27%; (b) 6½% approx. (iv) If only V affected in the same year, then V = –6%, P = 12%, T = 2% approx.

6.2 Lorry drivers (i) T grew. P levelled off. M grew less. MV = PT, therefore V was higher. (ii) M sets P two years later: (a) 9%; (b) 10%. (iii) Increased productivity, or rise to full employment. (iv) Fall in interest rates raises investment.

6.3 Bank of England (i) January, May (most special deposits). (ii) The Bank of England buys securities, and sells less. Price rises; real rate of interest falls. Diagram 3: 2 to 1. (iii) Buy short-term, and sell long-term securities, equally. (iv) Diagram 1, section 7.1, applied to the market for Treasury Bills, from 2 to 1. Price falls, so real rate of interest rises. (v) (a) Higher cost of borrowing, so it discourages investment; (b) cuts money supply and injections, so deflationary.

7.1 Look out for the boom (i) World distribution of income moves against developed countries. (ii) Must have been increased world money supply, some time earlier. (iii) Monetary policy; fiscal policy. (iv) Diagram 1, section 4.3; at level 1. (v) Income increased beyond 'full capacity level', so causing an inflationary gap.

7.2 Attack on inflation (i) If international competitiveness is lost. (ii) If lending from abroad, or to the government, is deterred completely. (iii) Oil is used in the production of all goods, and cannot be replaced – unlike olive oil. (iv) P rises, MV unchanged, so T falls; a world slump in output results. (v) Deflationary policies cut demand for goods and labour.

7.3 Simple sums (i) More borrowing, so more sales of securities: diagram 1, section 7.2, applied to the market for securities, from 2 to 1; price falls, real rate of interest rises. (ii) Tax cuts, in diagram 2; 2 to 1. (iii) If it increased national income beyond the level needed for full employment. (iv) Output, employment, growth are all less. (v) Expectations of future earnings from investment become impossible to assess.

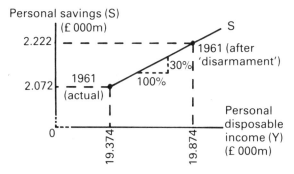

Diagram 1

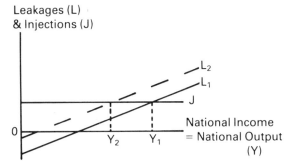

Diagram 2

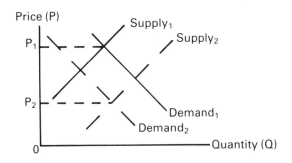

Diagram 3

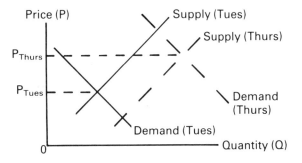

Diagram 4

Sources

Rae, G. (Sykes, E. *rev.*), *The Country Banker* (Pentagon Books) 1976, pp. 206-210: Letter XXIX 'Banking Finance'

5.3 'Cash Flow Problems'
Clarkson, G. P. E. and Elliott, B. J., *Managing Money and Finance* (Gower Press) 1972 (2nd ed.), pp. 22, 35, 36

'A Money Market Drama'
The Financial Times 13.2.78

6.1 '1970-77'
Lord, R., *The Daily Telegraph* 30.10.78

6.2 'Lorry Drivers' Test Run'
Lord, R., *The Daily Telegraph* 22.1.79

7.1 'After the Slump, Look Out for the Boom'
Crawford, M., *The Sunday Times* 23.5.76

7.2 'Attack on Inflation: A Policy for Survival' (HMSO) 1975

7.3 'If only Denis *did* Know Some Simple Sums'
Alexander, A., *Daily Mail* 14.11.78

2.1 'Away From It All?'
McLaughlin, E. & T., *Cost Effective Self-Sufficiency or The Middle-Class Peasant* (David & Charles) 1978 pp. 7-10

'The Merits of High Wages'
Cary, J. 'An Essay on the State of England in Relation to its Trade, its Poor, and its Taxes for Carrying on the Present War against France' (Bristol 1695) as quoted in Thirsk, J. and Cooper, J. P. (eds) *Seventeenth Century Economic Documents* (OUP) 1972, p. 321

2.2 'Disarmament'
Economic Intelligence Unit, *The Economic Effects of Disarmament* 1963, pp. 152-4

'Why the World Must Spend its Way out of Trouble'
Crawford, M., *The Sunday Times* 10.2.74

2.3 'Back to Industrial Investing?'
Green, M., *The Daily Telegraph* 19.6.78

'Tractors'
The Financial Times 8.3.78

3.1 'A Modest Revival in Output'
'Economic Outlook', *Midland Bank Review* May 1977, p.3

'The Kenyan Coffee Boom'
The Nation: Economic Report 1978-79 (Kenya) 1978

3.2 'Does It Pay?'
McLaughlin, E. & T. *op. cit.*, pp. 250-53

4.1 'The Future for Jobs'
Hamilton, A., *The Observer* 22.4.79

4.2 'Automation'
Blake, D., *The Times* 13.7.78

4.3 'Big Deal'
Punch 3.9.75, pp. 372-3

5.1 'Free from Cares'
Club Mediterranée, *Holiday Brochure* 1979

5.2 'The Country Banker'

Index